PRAISE FOR CONRAD SCHMIDT'S
Workers Of The World, Relax

"Human society, like the Titanic, is headed for a serious collision. Unless we change our ways of thinking about consumption and resource use, unless we demand that government provide really sustainable solutions, we, as a society and species, are headed for disaster. According to the latest UN report, we have only a few years to change our ways. Most political parties mouth the platitudes about sustainability, but few examine the fundamental nature of the crisis we face. Conrad Schmidt, founder of the Work Less Party, tackles the questions of over-consumption and the future of society in his newest book, *Workers of the World, Relax*. The book, in brief, is a revolution in the making and a revolution worth joining and fighting for. In a series of brilliant essays, Schmidt addresses questions that most politicians fear to face and offers "thinking-outside-the-box" solutions. Readers beware: Schmidt will make you think and question things you have been trained to accept as received wisdom. This is dangerous, radical stuff. It might just help you save your world. Read it and be part of the solution, rather than part of the problem."

– Christopher A. Shaw, Ph.D, Professor, UBC

"A great job, easy reading, but a very serious book. Good economics, good politics, personal stuff. Buy this book, buy a few copies."

– Gene Coyle, Ph.D Economics

"Despite Schmidt's humorous comments, his book is anything but light and is an eye-watering kick in the crotch for anyone who believes the world economic system, and its twins – capitalism and globalization – is sustainable now or into the near future."

– Mathew Burrows. Georgia Straight

MORE PRAISE FOR CONRAD SCHMIDT'S
Workers Of The World, Relax

"In his modest but empowering 143 pages, Schmidt does not limit
himself to the role of doomsayer, a common pitfall in much activist writing. Instead he levels constructive criticism at the myriad of
problems facing our dangerously wasteful society and responds
with policy alternatives that are thoughtful, well-researched and,
most importantly, practical."

-Martin Twigg. BC Book World

"Conrad Schmidt shows that the lessons of history, the laws of
nature and the yearnings of the human heart take precedence
over the money monomania of the economists and the blandish-
ments of advertisers. It's time to re-assesss the role of industrial
work in our lives and in society. Schmidt's book is a brilliant
resource for initiating that re-assessment."

– Tom Walker. Director GPI Pacific

"*Workers of the World, Relax*! is short and sweet, an easy read that
won't take too much of your precious little leisure time, but will
help you understand why you have so damn little and why our
economic priorities in North America are unhealthy, unsustainable and making us more stressed and less happy. This clever
and timely handbook by the founder of Canada's irreverent and
irrepressible Work Less Party offers great ideas for a better life

– John de Graaf, US Coordinator, Take Back Your Time

"Within the pages of Schmidt's first book *Workers of the World, Relax*!
lies the most interesting, comprehensive, readily grasped and
sensible writings on economics I've ever run across in my own
research. Run, don't walk, to the nearest book store, read this
book and internalize the message as it may be the only way out
of the lethal financial and environmental mess we humans find
ourselves in.

– Betty Krawczyk. Author of Lock Me Up or Let Me Go.

WORKERS OF THE WORLD, RELAX

WORKERS OF THE WORLD, RELAX:

The Simple Economics of Less Work

BY CONRAD SCHMIDT

Published 2006
ISBN 0-9739772-0-5

Printed & Bound in Canada

9 8 7 6 5 4 3 2

ACKNOWLEDGEMENTS

IT IS IMPOSSIBLE to give enough thanks to all the people who volunteered countless hours to bring this creation into existence. This book and the credit for its creation belong to you all. What motivated us was a belief that we could make a difference or at the very least try. A special thanks goes to Michelle Vergeer who believed in me enough to be the editor. Thanks also to Dave Herbert who helped add humour and charm to the book, Andrea Schmidt for the layout and design, Chantal Morin without whose help the topics would never have been so cleverly connected and to Bruce O'Hara who kept me on track whenever I felt like giving up. Thanks also to Niki Westman, Christine Ellis, Kevin Stiller, Ena Schmidt, Michael Cretzman, Tom Walker, Bill Tubbs, Johnathan Skinner, Lindy Harrigan and Matthew Risling for all your suggestions, research, editing, patience and support. Thanks everyone for believing in me and the possibility of a better future.

CONTENTS

PREFACE

WRITING THIS BOOK has been an interesting challenge. I received a lot of encouragement from friends (and even publishers) to write, but the book they wanted is not the one you hold in your hands.

I am known as a progressive, grassroots activist with a flair for media theatrics. I know how to garner attention while conveying a message. When the United States began to bomb Afghanistan in 2002, I erected a large graveyard in downtown Vancouver to symbolize the killing of innocent people. In 2004, I organized the World Naked Bike Ride, the worlds first, to protest climate change. It was an incredible event that happened on the same day in 28 cities around the world. In 2003, I formed a political party called the Work Less Party, which ran in the provincial and civic elections of British Columbia. We are planning to run a candidate for prime minister in the next Canadian federal elections. I have organized protests, written plays and much more.

My supporters encouraged me to write another compendium of fun and colourful antics that often made headlines around the world. This is definitely not that book. This book, unlike any of the events I am known for, has no frills. It is not about me or really anything fun. It is about economics.

Behind every war I have protested or environmental crime I have rallied against was an ideology supported by reason and respected academics. It's easy for left-wing environmentalists to organize and rally against injustices and label our opposition as evil fascists. However, those we label as greedy and evil are probably not that different from ourselves. I know this is not a popular sentiment. It's easy to become engrossed in believing we are on a righteous mission to save the world, to not recognize the similarities between us and the people we perceive as opposition.

A pivotal point in my life took place during a rally against the occupation of Iraq in 2003, where at least 50,000 people united in opposition. Literally thousands of anti-Bush posters and t-shirts dominated the procession. Despite the success of the event, I sank into melancholy watching many drive away in their cars. There we were, thousands of us happily protesting a war fought to prevent the collapse of our oil-dependent society. Whether we liked it or not, the soldiers we seemed to hate were risking their lives so we could maintain our consumerist lifestyle. Even though our hearts were in the right place, the cold, cruel logic of a resource dependent culture could not escape the necessity of the war. What we had was passion, yet we lacked economics.

It is one thing to protest. It is another thing to offer constructive solutions. Organizing huge anti-war rallies, protesting against climate change and tearing down fences at anti-globalization rallies will only succeed if in addition we have solutions to offer. This is why, instead of writing a book about the events I planned and my accomplishments, I have decided to write a book on economics. It is not an exceptionally complicated book. It's simple enough for even the most intelligent of academics to understand.

–Conrad Schmidt

INTRODUCTION

FIFTY YEARS AGO incomes were on the rise, the Cleaver family epitomized the North American ideal of middle class, and robotic technology was being hailed as the solution to every economic and social ill. "Experts" of the era wondered smugly what future generations would find to occupy their time, as science and automation would supply their every need with a minimum of human effort. Would our work-prone society find meaning in life working only half a week? Would the arts flourish as never before? Would a highly educated and endlessly curious population create a culture more sophisticated than any before? Sadly, these flights of fancy have proved baseless. Present day economic conditions seem a world away from those pleasant fantasies.

What happened?
Technological innovation, combined with cheap energy supplies, increased industrial efficiency; industry was able to produce more goods and services with less labour. This presented us with an option. We could perform less industrial labour or continue to work hard while producing and consuming more. We chose the second option.

There are approximately seven billion people on the earth today. As the population continues to grow it is becoming clear that the planet is not as big as we once thought it to be; it is also becoming obvious that humans are wreaking havoc upon the environment. The big question we have been trying to solve for the past 100 years is, "how do we maximize production and produce more and more stuff?" The big question we now face is, "what do we do with all the junk and pollution we have created?" To make matters worse, we now seem more determined than ever to work harder and produce more stuff, which creates a bizarre paradox, we are proudly breaking our backs to decrease the carrying capacity of the planet.

So what is the solution?
A great beginning would be to reduce the industrial workweek.

We would consume less, produce less, work less, pollute less and live more. Providing that the remaining work be distributed among more people, an industrial slow-down could have the additional benefit of reducing unemployment. This is a simple concept which has not garnered much attention. This book, in five parts, will tackle the ideological constraints to environmental sustainability and prove how a reduced workweek can help solve many of our social and environmental problems.

Part 1: Definitions

In order to change our behaviour we must first change the way in which we look at work; specifically, we must stop looking at it solely in terms of earning an income. To develop a more comprehensive understanding of our social and environmental impact we need a definition of work that encompasses a wider range of equally essential activities. Learning, socializing, child rearing and other activities are valuable and health sustaining work. The fact that we do not get paid for these activities does not mean they are unimportant. We will then examine two case studies that demonstrate how the work we do defines the world we live in.

Part 2: How?

According to the United Nations millennium report, sixty percent of the planet's ecosystems are in substantial decline. How are we doing this to the planet?

Cheap energy, combined with technological innovations that have given us the ability to modify waterways, change global weather patterns, unearth deadly toxins and kill many other species, are a culprit. Although we are the driving force behind industrialization, it is energy that fuels this process.

There is a growing misplaced faith that clean renewable energy will save us. This is highly unlikely. Over the last two hundred years our energy sources have been getting cleaner, yet we are doing more damage to the planet.

Part 3: Why?

Why is it that the more technologically efficient we become, and the cleaner energy sources become, we still abuse our new found industrial capacity with more roads, cars, airplanes and a wide array of useless products? Part 3 is an investigation into the history and purpose of consumerism.

The greatest threat to the environment is not climate change, acid rain, mercury contamination, over fishing or pollution. All of these are symptoms of the stress created by a consumerist society on fragile ecosystems.

The symptoms cannot be cured without solving the cause: consumerism.

Part 4: Putting It All Together

If the advantage of consumerism is increased employment and industrial growth, then what is the advantage of industrial growth? Why are we working so hard to produce such a dizzying number of products that are clearly harmful to us and the planet? It is not, as many think, simply a matter of greed. This part of the book summarizes the ideological requirements of sustainability into what I call a sustainability equation.

Part 5: A Better World

How we balance the requirements of sustainability against the competitive advantages of continued industrial growth is going to be the biggest challenge of the 21st century. An industrial slowdown is not optional. It is either going to be forced on us by an ecosystem that can no longer support us, or by ourselves in an effort to improve our lives. Over the past 150 years economics has focused exclusively on how to expand the economy. In the 21st century the science of slowing down the economy will be the premier field of research.

Part 5 explains how many aspects of our lives have the potential to change for the better.

PART I
DEFINITIONS

CHAPTER 1
WORK, CONSUMERISM AND HAPPINESS

WHAT IS WORK? It is one of the many words in the English language that has multiple interpretations and meanings. Work can be a noun or a verb, referring to a place we acquire a paycheque or the functions we perform. Physicists delving into universal questions of motion and energy equate work as a measurement of force multiplied by distance.

Many of us believe we have separated our daily activities into two categories: work and leisure. The energy put forth for the purpose of earning a paycheque is categorized as work, whereas energy invested in "elective" activities is called leisure.

The word work often conjures images of huddling behind a computer screen in an office, typing away to the inane dictates of management; or perhaps we imagine a bricklayer neatly piling and cementing a wall; or a truck driver cursing traffic as he delivers neatly stacked boxes. We do not generally think of a group of children playing soccer, or young lovers going on a first date. This is where the true definition of the word work diverges from our association of drudgery.

To analyze work we must step out of the social framework that has defined work as the opposite of leisure. We need to clarify how we refer to work. The Oxford Dictionary has a rather lengthy definition. An excerpt describes work as, "the application of mental or physical effort to a purpose; the use of energy." With this in mind, let us examine some common leisure activities to find out if energy is used and mental or physical effort is purposely being applied.

Is work being done on a first date? Yes, both mental and physical effort is being exercised for a purpose. Work has been done in getting both individuals to the same physical location. Work has been done to arrange the meeting. Work is being done as they attempt to impress one another.

When kids are playing soccer is work being done? Yes, both

mental and physical effort are being exercised for a purpose. Work is not just something we do in a factory or an office cubicle.

Leisure?

What, then, is leisure? Leisure is defined as, "time at one's own disposal." During leisure we get to choose how we spend our time.

Two important points about leisure:

1) Leisure involves work. Whether kicking a ball or reading a book, work is a continuous cycle occurring in some form or another.

2) Leisure is a voluntary activity. It is how you decide to invest your energy and time.

It is common in our society to think of work as activity we do outside of leisure, pursuing a paycheque. Is this definition valuable?

The excerpt from the Oxford Dictionary is particularly apt in its recognition of work as an ongoing cycle. There is no need to assess whether or not work is being done. What must be assessed is if the work being done benefits us as individuals, as a society and as a species. This work must additionally be assessed on the merit of how efficiently it is being done.

When we classify work merely as something that happens in factories or cubicles we forget the important work of living.

Parents spending time to raise and teach their families are working. They are working to create a healthy future for not only their children, but also for their future.

When you cook a healthy meal you are still working. You are working to look after your own health, and, in doing so, working to improve the health of your community. By looking after your health you help society decrease healthcare expenditures.

When you take time to build relationships with your neighbours you are working. You are working at building community. Strong communities have been shown to contribute to higher rates of longevity.[1]

When you take time to read a book, or research current political matters, you are working. You are working to stay informed, and helping yourself decide how various candidates and policies work for or against your interests.

When you take time to get to know yourself, you are working. You are discovering many of the important tasks, adventures, and challenges your life presents. If you wait until retirement to find those things of true value to your identity, it is often too late.

By taking time to explore and enrich ourselves and our communities we help to build a wiser and healthier society. Increased longevity and reduced medical expenses are among the likely benefits of wiser, healthier communities. Such communities offer a better place to live, raise families, and . . . work.

For the last forty years we have worked increasingly longer and harder in factories and offices. One consequence is that we work less and less at other tasks required to live healthy, rewarding lives. These tasks, much more important than the pursuit of consumer products (most of which eventually come to reside in landfills), are effectively being deleted from our consciousness. The work we currently prioritize is making us miserable.

We are expending all of our energy in the pursuit of status symbols and redundant artefacts instead of enjoying and working at the simple pleasures that life has to offer.

Consumerism and Happiness

The North American workweek has been on the increase since 1970. Americans now work an average of 1972 hours a year. Canadians work an average of 1718 hours a year. Americans also work nearly nine full weeks (350 hours) longer per year than western Europeans.[2] In addition to an increase in productivity and work hours there has been growth in the population of both Canada and the United States. Canada, with a population of 32,805,000, is growing at an annual rate of around 0.9%, while the United States, with a population of almost 300,000,000, is growing at an annual rate of approximately 0.92%.[3]

More North Americans than ever before are working longer, more productive hours. The consequence is an exponential increase in the number of products being produced.

There is no question that we have infinitely more luxuries than our ancestors of even a few generations ago. We have hot running water, lights that come to life at a flick of a switch, cars that can reach 100 km per hour in 3.8 seconds and mobile telephones with miniature cameras. Technology and innovation have thrown us into a world where we can produce, market, and consume more products than ever dreamt of a hundred years ago.

Are we happier?
Medical evidence suggests not. Both the United States and Canada are caught in a depression epidemic. In 2000 there were 7.8 million Canadians diagnosed and treated for depression. This is up from 2.72 million diagnosed in 1993. According to the World Health Organization depression is expected be the second-leading cause of disability in the world by 2020, trailing heart disease.[4] Several studies, including the Lundy Study of Sweden, have shown a ten-fold increase in depression rates over recent decades. It is also well documented that suicide rates, especially among the young, have been increasing. Historical evidence suggests that suicide rates were substantially lower in pre-modern times than they are today.[5]

How can this be when we have so much stuff to fill our lives and make us happy?
Several studies from the University of Illinois and the University of Michigan suggest that happiness does not necessarily correlate to the amount of consumer products a person possesses. [6]

We are beginning to understand that what makes life more enjoyable and rewarding is a community with substantive relationships, as well as a healthy, nurturing, physical and social environment.[7] Friends and community play a more significant role in our happiness than mere physical assets. Populations surveys from several countries have shown that citizens of wealthy nations are not necessarily happier than citizens of poorer countries.[8] Professor Ed Diener of the University of Illinois has done extensive studies comparing subjective well-being (SWB) – the scientific definition for how people evaluate their lives – between citizens of different countries, and different socio-economic groups. Diener's research revealed no difference between the Forbes 400 list of the richest Americans, and Masai herdsmen of East Africa. Not only was there no positive correlation between financial well-being and subjective well-being, the research additionally demonstrated a negative correlation between subjective well-being and multimillion dollar lottery winners.[9]

A 2002 sixty-eight nation cross-comparison by Veenhoven and Kalmijn revealed that poverty did not necessarily correlate to happiness. Ghana was one of the three poorest among the 68 countries surveyed, yet had one of the highest levels of reported happiness. Columbia was tied for happiest, yet was the 25th poorest. Austria, France and Japan were some of the richest nations in the study, yet reported below-average levels of perceived happiness.[10]

Today we are dedicating more and more of our lives to produce more and more consumer goods. We work harder toward the empty pursuit of producing goods than we do toward the fulfilling work of living. The harder we work to make and afford "stuff," the less time we have to enjoy our lives, spend time with friends and build healthy relationships and communities. We are neglecting aspects of our lives, essential to our well-being, in favour of status and material wealth accumulation that makes us no happier.

Our perverse work ethic is not just a social problem. The work we do affects the environment around us. The environmental tragedy of global warming, pollution and the extinction of millions of species are linked to the behaviour of our consumerist society. We are working longer and harder at decreasing the ability of our planet to sustain us, and less at doing the work of enjoying life.

So what is the solution?
Peculiarly enough, the current business and government sanctioned solution seems to be to encourage people to 'take a pill for it.' Today the antidepressant industry has grown to a 20 billion dollar a year industry. [11]

There is some contention that this industry is self-created by the pharmaceutical industry encouraging doctors to diagnose patients with depression more regularly.[12] There might be some truth to this, however, I believe that there is a real feeling of desperation affecting the majority of our lives. Antidepressants have been marketed since the 1960's, yet their monumental success is a fairly recent phenomenon. The industrial work week in North America has been increasing since the 1950's. The more we dedicate our time to trying to earn more, the less we have for the good work that rewards us. We know that healthy community and social relationships are essential to our happiness, yet we are dedicating less time to these activities and more time to producing more consumer goods that are not making us happier. This is not just an isolated personal issue. Happiness and self-satisfaction also come from pride in the work we do and the goals we aim for. As we start to take responsibility for our part in the industrial work of producing more and more consumer goods, it becomes increasingly difficult to take pride in work that is damaging the planet.

We are not as separated and isolated from the world as we might think. Social suffering, global warming and the extinction of millions of species are all depressing topics. Antidepressants have become a 20 billion dollar a year industry because there is a lot more to be depressed about. Denying the reality of our situation creates an inner conflict, which manifests unhealthy behaviours.

So will happy pills solve the problem?
Research suggests not.

Current clinical trial data on the relative risk of suicidal acts relating to the use of antidepressants in either children or adults points to comparable elevations in the risk of suicide.[13] Even the United States Food and Drug Administration now requires antidepressant drugs to be labelled as causing suicidal tendencies in children and teenagers. The United Kingdom has already banned prescriptions to children under the age of 18.[14]

Antidepressants are drugs that help people ignore problems. They are not a cure.

Notes

1. The connection between longevity and building healthier communities is known as the "Roseto Effect" in public health circles. For more information on the "Roseto Effect," please read Appendix D.

2. OECD, Organisation for Economic Co-operation and Development. Statistical Annex of the Employment Outlook. July 15 2004.

3. Central Intelligence Agency. CIA World Fact Book. 2005. ISSN 1553–8133. The CIA publishes The World Factbook in print and Internet versions. The World Factbook can be accessed at: www.cia.gov/cia/publications/factbook/index.html.

4. Heemann, Eve. Geropsychiatric And Mental Health Nursing. Jones and Bartlett Publishers, 2005. Page 131.

5. Schumaker, John F. The Age of Insanity: Modernity and Mental Health. Westport, CT: Praeger/Greenwood, 2001. Page 51–53.

6. Ed Diener, a University of Illinois psychologist, performed an extensive study comparing various focal groups from different social backgrounds. The study attempted to measure 'subjective well-being' which is defined as how a person evaluates his or her own life. There was a negative correlation between subjective well being and multimillion dollar lottery winners. He also found the lottery winners experienced higher rates of divorce, alcoholism, loss of friends and isolation:

Diener, Ed, Eunkook Suh, and Shigehiro Oishi. Recent Findings on Subjective Well-Being. University of Illinois. www.psych.uiuc.edu/~ediener/hottopic/paper1.html.

The relation between income and happiness is intricate. Although money is not a major source of the individual differences in well-being in wealthier nations, it can make a substantial difference in poor societies where basic needs are not fully met. Materialism, valuing money more than other things such as relationships, is usually a negative predictor of well-being.

A 16 nation study conducted by University of Michigan researcher Ronald Inglehart in 1980s showed very similar results.

Additional papers written by Ed Diener:

Diener, E., & Diener, C. (1995). The wealth of nations revisited: Income and quality of life. Social Indicators Research, 36, 275–286.
Finds that wealthy nations surpass poor ones on virtually every measure of quality of life:

Diener, E., Sandvik, E., Seidlitz, L., & Diener, M. (1993). The relationship between income and subjective well-being: Relative or absolute? Social Indicators Research, 28, 195–223.
Presents findings suggesting that the effects of income on happiness are not invariably relative to the income of others, as is often suggested :

Diener, E., Horwitz, J., & Emmons, R. A. (1985). Happiness of the very wealthy. Social Indicators Research, 16, 263–274.
Explores the subjective well-being of extremely rich Americans, and finds that they are only slightly happier than average Americans:

Diener, E., & Biswas-Diener, R. (2002). Will money increase subjective well-being? A literature review and guide to needed research. Social Indicators Research, 57, 119–169

7. Layard, Richard. *Happiness.* Penguin Books, 2005. Page 62–63.

8. Ibid, page 32–33.

9. Diener, E., & Diener, C. *The wealth of nations revisited: Income and quality of life.* Social Indicators Research, 36, 275–286. Dr Diener's website: www.psych.uiuc.edu/~ediener.

10. Ruut Veenhoven and Wim Kalmijn. Journal of Happiness Studies, Special Issue on 'Inequality of Happiness in Nations' 2005, Vol.6. Page 421–455.

11. Healy, David. *Let Them Eat Prozac: The Unhealthy Relationship Between the Pharmaceutical Industry and Depression*. New York: NYU Press, 2004. Page 52.

12. Ibid, p. 52.

13. MD Leslie Lundt, MD Marnin Fischbach. *Think Like a Psychiatrist*. Foothills Foundation, 2005. Page 63.

14. Boseley, Sarah. *The Guardian UK*. Prozac must have suicide warning: US to insist risks for children are spelt out on all antidepressants. September 15, 2004.

CHAPTER 2
TALE OF A DIAMOND

A diamond mine, 300 kilometres northeast of Yellowknife and 200 kilometres south of the Arctic Circle in the Northwest Territories, Canada.

THE TALE OF a diamond is but one in a larger book delineating the development of global capitalism and its effects on human society and thought. The tale of a diamond illustrates the power of an object arbitrarily valued by humans, and the lengths we will go to gain this power. The tale of a diamond is a tale of environmental destruction in the name of economic growth. It is a story of an entire nation forced into servitude; how the death of community was brought about by the greed of a few. The tale of a diamond does not have a happy ending, it leads to our current state. But, as with all worthwhile stories, we can learn from it and catch glimpses of the future.

The tale of a diamond begins simply enough with a question of definition. What is a diamond? The simple answer is that it is nothing but a hard, shiny stone.

Diamonds have a number of industrial applications; however, over 66 percent of their net sales are for use in jewellery. Diamonds are prized for their ornamental value despite the fact that man-made diamonds can easily be replicated at a significantly reduced cost and are virtually indistinguishable from natural ones.[1] It is logical then to assume that purchasers of diamonds are not buying them purely for aesthetic properties. As there is a substantial markup and a limited market for secondhand jewellery, it is also fair to conclude that diamond jewellery is not generally purchased for investment purposes. Therefore, diamonds must have some other value.

Once again, what is a diamond? One possible answer, in a social context, is that it is a hard, shiny stone that has a value to people beyond itself. They want it. It is status. It is wealth.

In 2003, rough diamond production accounted for $9 billion US, and diamonds purchased for polishing amounted to $11.8 billion US. The value of these polished diamonds was $14.8 billion US, with diamond jewellery retail sales of $61 billion US.[2]

This wealth creation comes at a huge environmental cost. Pipe mining, the most common and productive type of diamond mining, is a type of open pit mining that causes extensive environmental stress. On average, 40 to 250 tons of ore are excavated to find one stone large enough to polish into a single carat diamond.[3] In the process of moving this large quantity of ore, (to obtain a diamond with an approximate diameter of 6.5 mm) large areas and surrounding ecosystems are severely disturbed.

Acid mine drainage[4] contaminates water systems and consequently devastates surrounding wildlife areas. Unfortunately for certain diamond-rich places, such as parts of Sierra Leone and other West African regions, there is little infrastructure in place to enforce any environmental regulations. In these regions, in addition to the human costs associated with "conflict diamonds," [5] the environmental toll of mining operations can be steep. Pits are left open, and loose fill is left unmanaged to run off into rivers and streams, often with catastrophic effects.

So really, what is a diamond?

A hard, shiny stone that serves primarily as a status symbol for the owner, produced and purchased with little, if any, regard for the environmental devastation it causes.

Again, that is not all. We now move on to the bulk of the tale.

In 1867, the world's largest diamond fields were discovered in a small area, sparsely populated by a few thousand people, in a territorial division of the Cape Province in the Union of South Africa.

The apartheid regime of South Africa is one of the many sad instances of human repression in the 20th century. Apartheid was a series of legislative reforms that segregated the population and forced the non-white segment into servitude.[6] The most significant of these reforms were the *Land Act* of 1913 and the *Hut and Poll Tax* of 1848.[7]

The direct translation of the Afrikaans word apartheid means "to separate." School children were sent to separate schools. Non-whites had separate doctors, dentists and hospitals, all of which received substantially less funding. Interracial marriages were prohibited and non-whites could not own property in the same neighbourhoods as whites. They were forced to carry identity documents restricting movement to certain areas. The list of legislative reforms delegating non-whites to inferior status was virtually endless. [8]

Apartheid was not only an enforced ideological supremacy, but it was also a legislative and socio-political mechanism to ensure a cheap labour supply for South Africa.[9] During apartheid, South Africa was the world's largest producer of diamonds, gold, and uranium, and the second largest exporter of coal and copper. South Africa is also one of the world's richest sources of minerals.[10] In the pursuit of these precious resources, the ruling business class, and their eager-to-please counterparts in political office, found their biggest challenge. How could they coerce the indigenous population, who previously maintained a relatively sustainable and leisurely existence, into relinquishing community-based lifestyles in favour of spending thousands of hours underground. The problem that they faced was that the indigenous population had a very different value system.

Imagine you are an African farmer or hunter in the 18th century. Your home is beautiful and fertile. Days are filled with hunting trips and tilling the soil; evenings are filled with leisurely pursuits, maybe a little romance, storytelling, and dancing. Private ownership of land is unimaginable; people grow food for the community as a whole. The tasks of everyday life are communal efforts: some members plant seeds, some hunt or make tools, while others care for children.

It was by no means an idyllic world. It had its fair share of problems. Wars were fairly common and wealth accumulation was still part of their social structure. However, money was not used as a representation of wealth and the cruel cost of working in a mine did not outweigh the benefits. The indigenous population, for the most part, were not willing to sacrifice their way of life for financial resources of little real value.[11]

The demand for labour to work in the mines was so intense that the government even lifted the ban on selling guns to non-whites. Guns were the one white commodity that the indigenous population did have a practical use for. This increased the supply of labour, put the non-white population in a better position to resist further encroachment into their territories and thus, the ban was reinstated.

Unfortunately, the discovery of diamonds was only the beginning of the demand for labour. Gold, coal, plutonium, and many other mining operations followed. The challenge of industry and their political counterparts was to ensure a stable and cheap migrant labour force drawn from a reluctant population.

Conditions in South African diamond and gold mining industries were grotesque. By 1888, the death rate among the migrant non-white labour force rose to about 8 percent.[12] Black mine workers were locked in compounds for the duration of their contract. They were routinely stripped and given full body cavity searches. They were poorly compensated for their labour. Sixty-nine thousand mine workers died in accidents between 1900 and 1993, and more than one million were seriously injured. For any sane individual to give up a life of leisure, family, and African sunsets in exchange for one of the most miserable existences, you can be sure that they had to be amply persuaded.

Persuasion came in the form of a series of legislative reforms and land seizures. The hut and poll tax, which had to be paid in South African currencies, was introduced. Various laws were drafted which prohibited blacks from earning money through the sale of agricultural surpluses. Land was seized through raids and various legislative reforms, such as the 1913 *Land Act* which prohibited blacks from owning land outside designated areas. The effect was sweeping: 90 percent of the land was reallocated to the white minority, which made up only 13 percent of the population. In 1948, apartheid legislation was introduced that further stripped the black population of the possibility of having anything greater than a life of servitude to white masters.

A pivotal election in 1948 cemented the fate of blacks. Under the guise of "cultural preservation," the conservative Nationalist Party instituted the *Population Registration Act of 1950*, which demanded ethnic assignment at birth, and the *1954 Native Resettlement Act*, controlling the movement of blacks, where limited access was granted to restricted areas.

As a consequence of apartheid, the mines got labour, business boomed, and young couples all around the world were able to afford shiny diamond wedding rings. Energy plants were supplied with cheap coal and inexpensive high-grade uranium was mined for nuclear reactors and atomic bombs. Business was not just good for rich mining corporations, such as De Beers and Anglo America; business was good for the world. It is not so ironic that when sanctions were eventually introduced against South Africa, simple luxury goods such as television sets were mainly affected. None of the core industries (diamonds, steel, uranium, coal and gold, which were driving forces behind apartheid) were apartheid) were significantly affected. According to the American Committee on Africa, only 25 percent of all trade between the U.S. and South Africa was affected. Iron, steel, and, until late 1989, half-finished uranium continued to be imported.[13] The success of the apartheid regime was well appreciated throughout the world – its beneficiaries being, for the most part, the same people who condemned its implementers as evil fascists.

The struggle of the black people eventually succeeded in overcoming the white-only Apartheid government. A new government lead by Nelson Mandela and the ANC (Africanist National Congress) was elected in April 1994. In 1995 the new government set up a committee to expose the crimes of the apartheid government. This committee was called the truth and reconciliation committee. After several trials of both politicians and businessmen they produced a very revealing account of the history of apartheid that identified the mining industry as playing a central role in helping to design and implement apartheid policies.[14]

There are several aspects of apartheid that make its study so interesting in the light of labour investment:

1) It represents a relatively short space of time, during which a communal, tribal way of life transitioned into a non-sustainable system, dependent on the utilization of a finite amount of mineral resources. Those who invested labour were not the ones to benefit. In fact, a diamond had no value to the people who mined it. They would have had a higher quality of life if they had not been forced into mines, reluctantly accepting Western industrialization. Even today, not much has changed in South Africa. There is a strong economy standing to profit from a cheap mining labour force, which still exists.[15] Ten years after apartheid has ended, only a small percentage of the land was returned to the indigenous population. The government changed, but the motives and persuasion of capitalism did not.

2) Standard of living. How do we measure standard of living? If we were to measure the standard of living in a strict financial sense, the standard of living of the mineworkers would have been higher even though their life expectancy, leisure time, and overall

freedom had substantially decreased. I will return to the confusing topic of measuring standard of living in later chapters.

So what happened to apartheid? Moreover, what is the lesson history has given us?

The same driving forces that created and ended apartheid are not so different from the factors influencing the direction and investment of labour in the modern day industrialized world.

The South African apartheid government believed they could subjugate the indigenous black population by creating a strong police force, judicial system and army with an unscrupulous mandate to use whatever means necessary to enforce the discipline of the indigenous population to the biased laws created by the government. It did not work.

If you excommunicate a segment of the population from the benefit of common resources, you cannot expect the disenfranchised to respect property ownership and laws of the community. In other words, the crime rate went up exponentially.[16] Crime rates correlate to the degree of disenfranchisement from community resources experienced by the population. Once the apartheid government in South Africa was overthrown, crime rates continued to increase, the reason being that underlying issues were not being addressed.[17]

The second reason why law enforcement as a solution to civil disobedience did not work was because of organized resistance by the disenfranchised segments of society; community movements such as the African National Congress, Umkhonto we Sizwe (Spear of the Nation) and the Pan Africanist Congress. These organizations facilitated thousands of protests, uprisings and acts of sabotage.

The similarity between the two reasons is one of community resistance. An increase in crime rates is a reflection of inequality created by unjust laws and philosophies. It means that there is something wrong in the community. Yes, governments can make laws, police can enforce them, but it does not mean that those laws represent the interests of the community as a whole and it does not mean that the people who enforce these laws will be respected. High crime rates indicate distress.

No matter how aggressive and cruel the apartheid government of South Africa was, they were never able to steal the feeling of community that existed in the First Nations people of South Africa. Even though their land was robbed from them and the law relegated them to second-class citizens, they still had the most important and essential seed of change – community. It was this seed that helped them to work together and challenge injustice, which will hopefully aid them in addressing the fundamental causes of apartheid, namely the economic benefits of having an underpaid labour force working blindly to fuel industrial growth.

Identical problems exist worldwide. We are starting to recognize that our current industrial lifestyle is not sustainable. The western world operates on the assumption that we need to own a wide array of material goods; we operate on the assumption that industrial work is good. We no longer know how to share and interact with each other in the broader context of community. Private ownership of property is all that makes sense to us. To make matters worse, the harder we work, the worse things seem to become. Crime rates are increasing, climate change is causing billions of dollars of damage and we are exhausting cheap energy supplies.

As a society, we are going to have to ask ourselves why we are so committed to this course of reshaping the surface of the earth into an unsustainable wasteland. If we are going to complete the missing pieces of the puzzle, we must retrace our steps back to communities that were once sustainable, communities that understood the concept of sharing and working together, learn from them and retain some of the benefits our current society has to offer. It is not necessary for us to go back to living in mud huts and caves, but it is necessary for us to start caring about more than filling landfills with marvelous new technological wonders. We need a confluence of technological and social evolution that defines growth in terms of real sustainable development. This book is about questioning our current direction of labour, and proposing new approaches to valuing our labour.

The story of South African apartheid may, for many, seem like a distant world, but in truth it is not as distant from our own identity as we might think. The first cultural victim of Western industrial competitiveness was not in Africa or Latin America, but rather the transition we imposed upon ourselves. Today, as we head off to offices and factories with a committed determination to produce and consume, the first victim is our own spirit of individuality. The journey we engage in through the path of life is one of learning and social growth. If we single-mindedly focus on our purpose in this world as cogs in industrial machinery then we are denying the opportunity of essential social evolution.

Part of the purpose of reducing the workweek to more sustainable levels is to allow people that essential time and opportunity to engage in experiences that help us grow. We need to start defining work as more than what happens in offices and factories; we need to see the value of our labour as an investment in our life's energy to evolve and achieve meaning and purpose in our existence in this world. The first step to achieving this is redefining what we mean by the word 'work'.

Notes

1. Davis, Joshua. "The New Diamond Age". *Wired Magazine*. September 2003.

2. 2005 Diamond Industry Report. *Diamond Facts*. Published by Department of Industry, Tourism and Investment, North West Territories, Canada. Page 5.

3. Taku, Thomas A. *Framework for Industrialization in Africa*. Westport, CT: Praeger/Greenwood, 1999. Page 114.

4. Evangelou, V. P. *Pyrite Oxidation and Its Control: Solution Chemistry, Surface Chemistry, Acid Mine Drainage*. Boca Raton, FL: CRC Press, 1995. Page 1.

Acid mine drainage, sometimes referred to as AMD, results when the mineral pyrite (FeS_2) is exposed to air and water, resulting in the formation of sulphuric acid and iron hydroxide.

5. "Conflict diamonds are diamonds that originate from areas controlled by forces or factions opposed to legitimate and internationally recognized governments, and are used to fund

military action in opposition to those governments, or in contravention of the decisions of the Security Council." United Nations Organisation <www.un.org/peace/africa/Diamond.html> *Conflict Diamonds: Sanctions and War.* United Nations Department of Public Information in cooperation with the Sanctions Branch, Security Council Affairs Division, Department of Political Affairs.

6. Sporton, Deborah and David S. G. Thomas. *Sustainable Livelihoods in Kalahari Environments: Contributions to Global Debates.* Oxford, UK: Oxford University Press, 2002. Page 42. M.

7. Although the apartheid government used the term apartheid to refer to segregationist laws passed from 1948, the term has came to refer to all the laws that subjugated the indigenous population. The *Land Act of 1913* was by far the most significant.

8. Donnelly, Jack. *International Human Rights.* Boulder, Colorado: Westview Press, 1997. Page 64-65.

9. Lowenberg, Anton D. and William H. Kaempfer. *The Origins and Demise of South African Apartheid: A Public Choice Analysis.* Michigan: The University of Michigan Press, 1998. Page 5.

10. Arnold, Guy. *The New South Africa.* New York, NewYork: St. Martin's Press, 2000. Page 91. M.

11. Waetjen, Thembisa. *Workers and Warriors: Masculinity and the Struggle for Nation in South Africa.* Illinois: University of Illinois Press, 2004. Page 41.

12. Simons, Jack and Ray. *Class & Colour in South Africa 1850-1950.* Harmondsworth, Eng: Penguin Books, 1969. Chapter 2.

13. Chomsky, Noam. *Detering Democracy.* Hill and Wang, 1992. Page 239.

14. Vol. 4, Ch. 2 of the Truth and Reconciliation Committee (TRC) "Institutional Hearing: Business and Labor." Findings Arising out of Business Sector Hearings. 15 December 2004.

15. Although the law of apartheid officially ended when Nelson Mandela became President of South Africa, the fundamental causes have never been addressed. Poverty and inequality actually

increased after Nelson Mandela became president. A recommended paper to read on this topic is:

Hoogeveen, Johannes G. Not Separate, *Not Equal: Poverty and Inequality in Post-Apartheid South Africa*. William Davidson Institute at the University of Michigan. Berk Özler.

> "As South Africa conducts a review of the first ten years of its new democracy, the question remains as to whether the economic inequalities of the apartheid era are beginning to fade. Using new, comparable consumption aggregates for 1995 and 2000, this paper finds that real per capita household expenditures declined for those at the bottom end of the expenditure distribution during this period of low GDP growth. As a result, poverty, especially extreme poverty, increased. Inequality also increased, mainly due to a jump in inequality among the African population. Even among subgroups of the population that experienced healthy consumption growth, such as the Coloureds, the rate of poverty reduction was low because the distributional shifts were not pro-poor."
> … "Not Separate, Not Equal:Poverty and Inequality in Post-Apartheid South Africa".

16. Crime correlations with inequality found in:

Kaplan, George et al. *Inequality in Income and Mortality in the United States: Analysis of Mortality and Potential Pathways*. British Medical Journal, Vol. 312, No. 7307: April 20, 1996. Page 999–1003.

For a related study correlating inequality to mortality rates see:

Kennedy, B.P., Kawachi, I., and Prothrow-Stith, D. *Income Distribution and Mortality: Cross Sectional Ecological Study of the Robin Hood Index in the United States*. British Medical Journal, Vol. 312, No. 7307: April 20, 1996. Page 1004–1007.

Although absolute poverty levels do not significantly correlate with the crime rate , income inequality does. Two separate

studies, one from Harvard, the other from Berkeley, compared
state crime rates to their income inequality rates, and found
that the states with the most inequality had the highest rates of
homicide, violent crime and incarceration.

17. Hoogeveen, Johannes G. *Not Separate, Not Equal: Poverty
and Inequality in Post-Apartheid South Africa*. William Davidson
Institute at the University of Michigan. Berk Özler.

CHAPTER 3
THE RISE AND FALL OF THE STONE ECONOMY

Stone statues on Easter Island

OUR CONNECTION TO the planet is fractured, and we must come to realize that our abusive consumption directly affects our mental and physical health. Environmental sustainability offers a most persuasive argument in favour of the work of living and less industrial work.

Every day the media tells us of new environmental disasters and potential threats to the human race: global warming, overfishing, water pollution, pesticide contamination, influenza epidemics, new antibiotic-resistant super bugs, natural resource depletion, acid rain, overflowing landfills, plus countless forms of air and water-born toxins. Even though this list seems dauntingly long and complex, it is essential we recognize all the above threats as symptoms of the same problem.

The problem is not toxic leakage from landfills, gulf streams collapsing or global warming; it is the inability of the planet to withstand the pressures of a consumerist society in a fragile eco-system. As long as our society is bent on expanding the industrial economy and attempting to discover uses for a long list of products we don't really need, the planet will not be able to sustain us.

This is not the first time a civilization has directed the efforts of its labour in a manner which has reduced the carrying capacity of their environment. It has been the downfall of many civilizations. The most famous example is Easter Island, from 690 AD to 1800 AD.[1]

The story of Easter Island, and its significance as a social and environmental parallel to modern day civilization, is well recognized. It serves as an interesting example and reminder of how our species exists not as a dominant force, but rather as a component in a complex network comprised of all living species on this planet, in a web of essential interdependencies.

Easter Island is over 2,000 miles from the nearest population centres, Tahiti and Chile, making it one of the most isolated places on the planet. The first European explorer to discover this triangular volcanic rock formation was Admiral Roggeveen, who came upon the island on Easter, 1722. What surprised Roggevenn was the existence of some 200 stone statues that lined the coast. Some were as high as 33 feet and weighted 82 tons. He also discovered an additional 700 statues in varying degrees of completion, some of which were as high as 65 feet and weighed 270 tons.[2] To put this in perspective, the Statue of Liberty in the United States weighs 220 tons and stands 150 feet tall. However, the Statue of Liberty was constructed by a civilization of several million people. The population of Easter Island, at the time of the construction of the statues, was approximately 7,000 and the island itself is only 46 square miles in size.[3] The construction of the statues was a mammoth investment of labour by the population and a very intense burden on the ecosystem. For a civilization to be able to achieve such an incredible feat, it is logical to assume that it was relatively advanced in technology and social architecture. However, the Easter Island that was discovered by Roggeveen had no great civilization: there were approximately 2,000 natives living mostly in caves and existing on a diet of rats and chickens. The island was barren with no timber for scaffolding, nor plants for making heavy rope. The few boats that they possessed were described as "bad and frail." [4]

What happened to this once great civilization able to create a social and technological order that allowed them not only the ability to create the statues, but also the time to invest their labour beyond mere subsistence living into creating a thriving civilization? The statues were not the only mark of social and technological development; their list of achievements is impressive. In addition to the statues, the community possessed the Rongorongo script, which is the only written language in Oceania. The island was also home to many wood and tapa (barkcloth) crafts, tattooing, string figures, dance, and music. Evidence also exists that a social order of cooperation and sharing existed.

Using techniques of radio carbon dating, earth core sampling, and examining trash pits from past inhabitants, archaeologists have been able to reconstruct a potential history of the de-evolution of both the island's ability to support humans and the disintegration of the culture that had achieved so much.[5] Core, grain, and pollen samples revealed that the island, discovered by the initial Polynesian settlers around 400 to 700 AD, was a sub-tropical paradise, rich in both plant and animal life. Thick forests of palm trees covered the hills. Other plants, including the hauhau tree which can be used to make ropes, were also numerous. Seabirds, such as the albatross and boobies, relied upon Easter Island as a nesting place.

By examining trash pits from various periods of the island's history, archaeologists have discovered that the primary diet of the islanders was sweet potatoes, chickens and marine life; primarily porpoise. The porpoises were hunted far offshore in sturdy hulled canoes made of wood. The advantage of this diet was that it was not very labour intensive and left plenty of time for other activities.[6]

The statues were status symbols used to trumpet the relative hierarchy of competing clans. The larger and more numerous the statues were, the wealthier the clan.[7] These symbols, just like many of the status symbols of today, were resource intensive.[8] In addition to trees being chopped down for domestic use, they were also used to make rollers and sledges to transport the statues. By 1400 AD, the hauhau trees were well on their way to becoming extinct. When there were no longer any trees left to cut down, there was no longer wood to make the heavy canoes needed to hunt porpoise. With the porpoises out of reach, the people had to turn to the seabirds and finally, to rats. Trees were also an essential component in maintaining the fertility of the soil. As a result of diminishing harvests, a loss of access to food and an expanding population, starvation resulted, the social order collapsed and cannibalism appeared. Human bones started to find their way into trash pits.

It's easy for us in 21st century to look back and criticize the inhabitants of Easter Island. Surely all they needed to do was stop building useless stone statues and reduce the strain on their ecosystem. Unfortunately it is not that simple. Today our society is in a very similar situation. The difference is that instead of useless statues we make millions of tons of consumer goods that for the most part end up in landfills. Its easy to assume that the solution is simply to just stop doing it, but is it?

Part of what drove technological and social development on Easter Island was an economy based upon the production of large statues. Trade was facilitated by resources being widely scattered on the island. The best stone for the statues came from one quarry, while the stones for the statues' crowns came from another, and the tools to work the stone yet from another location. Astronomy was encouraged to align the statues with constellations. Engineering, and a knowledge of physics, were encouraged by the complexity of moving and erecting the massive works.[9] The inhabitants of Easter Island built up one of the most advanced civilizations in Oceania.

A major part of what drives technological innovation in our society is mass production balanced by mass consumption. Each year new cars are being replaced with more efficient and advanced models. Yesterday's vacuum cleaners are being replaced by new robotic versions. Old 5k computers are being replaced with new 3 gig hertz machines. Demand for new innovative technologies is the primary driving force of most of the scientific research in our world. The Easter Island people were not just an advanced civilization that had nothing to do except build stone statues. The statues were in part what made them advanced and in part what destroyed their civilization.

To be able to solve the mystery of the requirements of sustainability we need to understand the motives behind why we created a consumer-based society. This topic will be further discussed in Part 3 of this book.

Occasionally, I wonder if there was an activist group 300 years ago on Easter Island, perhaps called Green Island or the Easter Island Conservation Society, that warned people that they were destroying their resource base. If they did exist, were they classified as radical left-wing activists who do not understand the pressures of the island stone carving economy? Stop carving statues, how am I to live? We can simply grow more trees!

Two Way Street

Even today, there are still many scientists and politicians who believe that environmental evolution is a two-way street. They should take a page out of history, because what the Easter Islanders did not realize was that once all the trees were chopped down, there would not be enough vegetation to keep the growth-essential topsoil in place. Once the topsoil washed away, there was no longer enough nutrition in the soil to re-grow trees. There was no turning back!

We are in a very similar situation. Every ecosystem and the biosphere as a whole represents a dynamic system of an infinite amount of factors maintaining balance. There is a point of human influence that once reached, there can be no turning back. One likely possibility is carbon dioxide sinks becoming carbon dioxide sources.

Carbon dioxide is the primary source of human pollution contributing to global warming. Every year we release 20 billion tons of carbon dioxide into the environment. Fortunately, substantially less than this amount makes it into the atmosphere. The ocean and forests act as carbon dioxide sinks. In other words, they absorb. However, once the planet reaches a certain temperature, the trees and the oceans are expected to start releasing carbon dioxide.[10]

A potentially even more serious threat than a carbon dioxide feedback is thousands of years of methane gas, which have been stored in permafrost ice across the world, being released into the atmosphere.

An international research partnership known as the Global Carbon Project in 2005 identified melting permafrost as a major source of feedbacks that could accelerate climate change by releasing greenhouse gases into the atmosphere. It has been reported and confirmed that western Siberian peat bogs, formed around 11,000 years ago, are melting. It is estimated that the west Siberian bog alone contains some 70 billion tonnes of methane, which is a quarter of all methane stored on the land surface worldwide. Methane is about twenty times more potent than carbon dioxide. Western Siberia is warming faster than almost anywhere else on the planet. It has had an increase in average temperatures of some 3 degrees Celsius in the last 40 years.[11]

Proof of climate changes on a local and global scale are becoming increasingly visible across the world. The ten hottest years in the global temperature record, now 143 years old, have now all been since 1990. According to the Meteorological Service of Canada, today's atmosphere contains 31 percent more carbon dioxide, one of the main greenhouse gases, than at the start of the industrial era.[12]

The Intergovernmental Panel on Climate Change (IPCC) which bases its assessments mainly on peer-reviewed and published scientific and technical literature from seven hundred of the world's leading climate scientists representing more than a hundred countries, released a disturbing report on the impacts of climate change. Impacts from climate change this century are expected to be extensive, and in some cases, severe. Some countries can expect a reduction in crop yields and an increase in drought, while others may experience an increase in flooding. The report also notes natural systems, like coral reefs and other sensitive areas, "may undergo significant and irreversible damage" due to climate change.[13]

In 2005 the United Nations released its Millennium assessment. This report on the environment represented the peer-reviewed work of over 1300 scientists from 95 countries. The assessment found that a majority of the Earth's ecosystems are in decline and that 90% of the large ocean fish are now gone.[14]

On February 16, 2005, the threat of global warming finally broke ranks from academic debate into a commitment by the governments of the world to take action. On February 16, 2005, the Kyoto protocol came into effect. The protocol is the commitment of nations to reduce their greenhouse gas emissions by 5.2%, compared to the year 1990. As of February 16, 2005, 141 nations have ratified the protocol.

Great! We now have an international commitment to reduce greenhouse gasses, but do we have a plan?

In April 2005, I attended a political party discussion forum on how to reduce our environmental footprint. That evening, both the Green Party and New Democrat Party had some of their best speakers in fine tune to present party line. I noticed that evening how both "environmentally progressive" parties were proposing very similar solutions. The fundamental ideology was that technology would come to the rescue; biodiesel, wind turbines, solar panels and hydrogen were not only going to save humanity, but make us rich at the same time. Green technology was allegedly going to be the fuel of a new industrial era of prosperity for us all – the best of both worlds. I have collected a substantial amount of promotional material from candidates of environmentally progressive political parties describing how they believe that it is possible to grow the economy and reduce our environmental footprint.

Despite the fact that the forum's key issue was environmental sustainability, none of the major political parties mentioned a reduction in production or consumption. In fact, the solutions they all proposed were pro-'green' businesses becoming engines of future growth.

With so many business representatives and politicians promoting 'green' technological solutions to our environmental problems, one might think that this is the only solution.

This is incorrect. We have the option of shrinking the industrial economies of the world. Work less, produce less and consume less. For most politicians, economists and the corporations that fund them, this strategy is regarded as either completely taboo or laughably ridiculous.

Is such an idea ridiculous ?
The millennium assessment scientists have warned us that we are potentially facing serious harmful consequences in the next 50 years. The only thing that is ridiculous is that the only strategy being discussed is one to reduce our environmental impact at the same time as growing the economy. Two potentially contradictory concepts. In the next section we will investigate why technology is intrinsically connected to a dependence on increased industrial output and consumerism.

Before we analyze some of the advantages and potential strategies of shrinking the industrial economy, an important first step is to take an honest reflection into why, with the increasing aid of technology, we have been working so hard to produce and consume so much.

Notes

1. Flenley, John and Paul Bahn. *The Enigmas of Easter Island: Island on the Edge.* New York: Oxford University Press, 2002. Page 75.

2. Ponting, Clive. *A Green History of the World.* Penguin Books, 1992. Chapter 1, The Lessons of Easter Island.

3. Mordo, Carlos. *Easter Island.* Firefly Books, 2002. Page 23.

4. Flenley, John and Paul Bahn. *The Enigmas of Easter Island: Island on the Edge.* Oxford University Press RRP, 2003. Page 159.

5. The explanation of the history of Easter Islands is by no means

fact. It is the current most accepted interpretation of the archea-logical evidence presented.

6. Ponting, Clive. *A Green History of the World*. Penguin Books, 1992. Chapter 1, The Lessons of Easter Island.

7. Flenley, John and Paul Bahn. *The Enigmas of Easter Island: Island on the Edge*. Page 111–112, 152.

8. Ibid. Page 123.

9. Mordo, Carlos. *Easter Island. Firefly Books*, Ltd, 2002. Page 113.

10. Researchers from the University of California and the U.S. Forest Service, measuring the amount of carbon dioxide flowing into and out of Alaskan tundra over five summers, published the first evidence of significant net emission. They calculate that if their results apply to the entire high latitude belt, the tundra emitted 0.19 billion tonnes of carbon in 1990, some three percent compared to all the carbon emitted from fossil fuel burning that year.

11. Pearce, Fred. "Climate Warning as Siberia Melts". *New Scientist Magazine*. August 11, 2005.

12. The Meteorological Service of Canada (MSC) was created in 1871 as one of the early acts of the new Government of Canada: Hengeveld, Henry, Elizabeth Bush and Patti Edwards. *Frequently Asked Questions About the Science of Climate Change*. Published by MSC. This paper was based on IPCC reports and recent peer-reviewed scientific papers.

> Since the Industrial Revolution began, concentrations of CO_2 have increased by about 31 percent, methane has more than doubled, and nitrous oxide has risen by 17 percent. There is clear evidence that these increases are mostly due to the burning of fossil fuels for transportation, heating and electricity and other human activities. Carbon dioxide accounts for about two thirds of the predicted increases in the greenhouse effect that these changes have caused to date.

13. IPCC Second Assessment Synthesis of Scientific-Technical Information relevant to interpreting Article 2 of the UN Framework Convention on Climate Change.

14. The website for the UN Millennium Assement is located at www.millenniumassessment.org.

PART 2

CHEAP ENERGY AND TECHNOLOGY: A LETHAL COMBINATION

Cheap energy has given us the ability to modify the planet to better suit our needs. We use energy to build more roads, build bigger cities, more airplanes, etc. Technology is what improves the efficiency with which we use energy. The greater our technology the more we can accomplish with less energy.

The more energy we combine with greater technology, the more damage we are likely to do to the biosphere.

It seems that we are now running out of cheap oil, the substance that has fueled industrial growth for the past 100 years. Is this a good or a bad thing?

A Canadian paper and pulp mill

CHAPTER 4
JEVONS' PARADOX

The lesson of history is that the cleaner and cheaper an energy source is, the more we are inclined to abuse it and damage the ecosystem of the planet.

THERE IS NO issue more critical to understanding the requirements of sustainability than understanding Jevons' Paradox. William Stanley Jevons was an economist who noted that "as technological improvements increase the efficiency with which a resource is used, total consumption of that resource may increase, rather than decrease."[1]

Jevons made this discovery with regard to the coal industry in 1865. The expectation during the 19th century was that the efficiency of steam engines would result in less coal consumption. Jevons realized that the more efficient the steam engine became, the more industry grew and the more coal was needed. The exact opposite of what was expected occurred.[2] Jevons' Paradox is not limited to automobiles; it encompasses our awkward relationship to resources, directly applicable to most aspects of industry and consumption.

A very clear past example of this problem was the 1975 CAFE standard. During the 1970s the price of oil rose to nearly $80 a barrel. High prices resulted in an increased demand for more efficient vehicles. The demand for efficiency was legislated in the Energy Policy and Conservation Act of 1975, which mandated an increase in the efficiency of automobiles. The overall goal was to increase fuel efficiency to 27.5 mpg by 1985.[3] The logic of the United States Congress was that more efficient vehicles would result in less fuel use overall and thus, save money. They were wrong. More efficient vehicles had a two pronged effect: more people driving and people driving more.

A study by Freund and Martin in 1993 found that although gasoline efficiency in the U.S. improved considerably (34%) between 1970 and 1990, total fuel consumption increased by 7%.[4]

When relative fuel prices began to diminish in the '80s,[5] economists expected that the decrease would help reduce demand for fuel. They were wrong. Lower fuel prices resulted in an increased demand for SUVs. SUVs typically consume 20% more fuel than a regular passenger vehicle. Net fuel usage continued to increase.

Jevons' Paradox and Industry

Productivity has been increasing exponentially for more than a century. An average worker needs to work a mere 11 hours per week to produce as much as one working 40 hours per week in 1950. This increase in productivity led many futurists to predict that work would become a less defining feature of our lives. There was even concern that we would not know what to do with all our new found leisure time.[6] Reality stands in stark contrast to those optimistic predictions. Today we are working longer and harder than we in the 1970s while producing more. Americans work 12% longer than they did in the 1970s.

How did this happen ?
Cheap energy and mechanization gives industry the ability to manufacture more goods and services with the same amount of labour. This gives us an option: we can either work less or consume and waste more. We chose the option of consuming and wasting more.

Jevons' Paradox and the Environment as a Resource

Many economists, politicians and environmentalists are determined to find new ways of building the economy by implementing new technologies which will reduce the per unit amount of damage created and thus, enable us to continue to grow. The 'green' movement is not a new concept. For the last century we have been searching for technological advancements for the purpose of reducing pollution. Cars were initially advertised as an environmental leap over "polluting" horses. Petrol was promoted as the environmentally friendly solution to coal, then nuclear was hailed as an improvement over petrol, and so on. The more we reduce the immediate impact of a technology or energy source, the more it enables us to use it to excess and ultimately, do more damage to the biosphere. It seems logical the more environmentally friendly the production technique is, the less damage will be done. Once again, Jevons' Paradox comes into effect and the exact opposite to what we expect occurs. The cleaner and more environmentally friendly production becomes, the greater the amount of environmental damage done. This is known as the rebound effect or Jevons Paradox.

A prime example is the paper and pulp mill industry, which use a wide range of highly toxic chemicals such as cyanide, arsenic, chlorine, mercury and lead. These chemicals, which, if not treated correctly, can have an immediate and dramatic impact on the local environment.[7]

There are countless documented cases of paper and pulp mills damaging local ecosystems. On October 17, 1994, an explosion at the mill in Powell River, British Columbia, ruptured a chlorine dioxide storage tank and released 600,000 liters of chlorine into the environment. In addition to killing aquatic life, many of the emitted pollutants have been linked to causing cancer in humans.[8]

Due to the easily visible effects of paper and pulp mill pollution, neighbouring residents and local officials have been quick to demand strict legislation enforcing environmental cleanup. Even banks and other financiers are insisting on more environmentally friendly production techniques.[9] Business has realized that a cleaner production technique will result in less resistance from local communities.

The paradox is that if our goal is to reduce our impact on the environment, it isn't working.

In 1970, the planet's paper production was approximately 126 million tons. In 1997, 298 million tons of paper were produced. About 40% of the world's industrial wood harvest is used to make paper.[10] Even in cases where only new growth forests are harvested, it still represents a substantial negative impact on the natural ecosystem. The majority of the 298 million tons of paper will be disposed of in toxic landfills, breaking the cycle of organic matter re-nourishing the earth. Paper accounts for approximately half of all the space in landfills in the US.[11] Newspapers consume 41,000 trees daily.[12] Per capita consumption of paper has increased from nearly 18 to 50 kg between 1950 and 1997.[13]

Why do more environmentally friendly production technologies increase overall production ?

Paper and pulp mills will release as many toxins into the environment as they can get away with. More environmentally friendly production techniques will not reduce pollution from pulp and paper mills, but rather increase the amount of pulp and wood they can process. The more environmentally friendly milling technologies become, the less damage done per unit of production. This enables more paper mills to process more trees.

In addition to increased long term effects, paper and pulp mills continue to pollute the immediate environment. Even though the amount of impact per unit of production has decreased, total production has more than doubled. Paper and pulp mills discharge

close to two million tons of toxic chemicals into Canadian waterways every day. Environment Canada reported over 3000 environmental violations by pulp mills in recent years.[14]

Notes

1. Manno, Jack. *Privileged Goods*. FL, USA: CRC Press LLC, 1999.
Page 185. .

2. Shah, Sonia. *Crude: The Story of Oil*. New York: Seven Stories
Press, 2004. Page 40.

3. Padgett, Marty. *Hummer: How the Little Truck Company Hit the
Big Time, Thanks to Saddam, Schwarzenegger, and GM*. MN, USA:
Motorbooks International, 2004. Page 29.

4. Manno, Jack. *Privileged Goods*. FL, USA: CRC Press LLC, 1999.
Page 185.

5. Bradsher, Keith. *High and Mighty: The Dangerous Rise of the SUV*.
USA: PublicAffairs, 2002. Page 37.

6. Rifkin, Jeremy. *The End Of Work*. New York: Putnam Books, 1995.

7. Ashok Pandey. *Concise Encyclopedia of Bioresource Technology*.
USA: Haworth Press., 2004. Page 145.

8. Johansen, Bruce Elliott. The Dirty Dozen Praeger/Greenwood,
30 June 2003. Page 184.

9. Clay, Jason W. *World Agriculture and the Environment: A Commod-
ity-By-Commodity Guide to Impacts and Practices*. Washington, DC:
Island Press, 2004. Page 325.

10. Brown, Lester Russell, Brian Halweil and Michael Renner. *Vital
Signs 1999: The Environmental Trends That Are Shaping Our Future*.
New York: W. W. Norton & Company, 1999. Pages 78–79.

11. Gore, Albert. *Earth in the Balance: Ecology and the Human Spirit.* USA: Houghton Mifflin Books, 2000. Page 151.

12. Hamelman, Steven L. *But Is It Garbage: On Rock and Trash.* USA: Publisher University of Georgia Press, 2004. Page 27.

13. Lester Russell Brown. *Vital Signs 2000.* New York:W. W. Norton & Company. Page 78.

14. Boyd, David R. *Unnatural Law: Rethinking Canadian Environmental Law and Policy.* Canada: UBC Press, 2003. Page 34.

CHAPTER 5

ENERGY: THE FUEL OF INDUSTRIALIZATION

The first law of the conservation of energy states: Energy cannot be created or destroyed, it can only be changed from one form to another.

IT TOOK BILLIONS of years for this little planet to evolve into a form we could recognize as Earth. It took another billion or so years for life to form and evolve, to differentiate into a vast array of billions of separate species, all living in an intricate web of interdependence, all in harmony with global patterns.

Suddenly, one species starting getting ideas.

This was not a problem in and of itself. Many animals are quite clever and all species were adept at doing what they needed to do to survive and propagate, even if that something was nothing at all. Even the efforts of this particular species to obtain food and create shelter were no more disruptive. We eventually discovered how to grow plants almost wherever we wanted and coax other animals to help maintain our crops. Tapping into ancient rivers assisted in these endeavors.

Still, the changes our ancestors made to their environment were relatively minor in scale; they farmed within the cycles of weather and harnessed animals adapted to domestic roles just as they had adapted to other outside influences.

Then, in an instant, geologically speaking, everything changed. Or, more accurately, this species changed everything. In barely a century, we went from living in relative harmony with our surroundings to drastically altering the environment. Some adjustments were intentional; most were not. We drained lakes, relocated others, altered the flow of waterways, replaced forests with barren fields, created holes in the atmosphere with the by-products of machines and factories and altered the natural drainage and absorption of rainfall with a concrete network of roads. We left strange and noxious chemicals everywhere, poisoning and mutating nearly every living thing, including ourselves.

How were we able to make such drastic changes in such a short time? We found a new source of energy and developed a way to harness it. We found coal and oil, the stored energy of the sun. We used these sources to fuel machines, machines to make life easier, which helped obtain fuels and use energy more efficiently. Our effect on the world grew exponentially, until, at the beginning of the twenty-first century, we stood atop a giant heap of styrofoam containers, obsolete electronic equipment, abandoned automobiles and mysterious chemical by-products, staring down with contempt at the remains of a planet of which we had once been an intimate part.

Despite what you may hear from pundits and doomsayers, there is no energy crisis, at least not in the way they imply. There is certainly no energy shortage. Energy is everywhere. It drives and crafts all life and matter on the planet. It is in the rays of the sun, the wind that circulates our atmosphere, even within the bonds of every atom.

The energy "crisis" is specific to one particular species: ours. Our renovation is not yet complete. There are still forests standing where we would like to grow feed for the livestock we consume. There are still wetlands to build condominiums in which to live. The minerals we need to build taller and taller skyscrapers are still buried. Unfortunately for humankind, though the other species may breathe a sigh of relief, we are running out of easily extractable energy.

Oil, the darling of modern times, is still plentiful. There are still trillions of tons scattered around this planet. It's getting at it that will become a problem. Peak oil is the term we use to describe the point after which we start extracting less and less oil per day, using current methods. One estimate of when we will reach this point between 2000 and 2010.[1] What other sources are available?

Coal

Coal is the 'dirtiest' of all the fossil fuels. It is the leading source of mercury contamination and a prevailing source of sulfur dioxide, carbon dioxide and particulate matter, all of which can cause serious health problems, including asthma, lung damage, cancer, cardiovascular disease, mutagenic effects and premature death.[2]

The National Academy of Sciences [3] estimates that every year in the United States, 60,000 children are born who may suffer brain damage and will consequently have difficulties academically because their mothers ate mercury contaminated fish.[4] According to the Environmental Protection Agency, more than 450,000 river miles in the United States are contaminated with dangerously high levels of mercury pollution.[5] The EPA also estimates that approximately 24,000 Americans die on average of fourteen years earlier due to exposure to power plant pollution. 2,800 of those deaths are from lung cancer. Health Canada estimates that air pollution kills 5900 Canadians a year.[6] Even though our supplies of cheap oil may only last another 10 years,[7] there is still potentially over a hundred years of coal left. What limits the ability of coal to sustain anticipated future growth is the highly toxic nature of coal pollution and secondly, it is a scarce resource whose prices are subject to demand and supply. The price of coal increased by 48% in 2004 and is expected to continue to rise.[8]

At the beginning of the 20th century, coal was the main energy source. The toxic chemicals released into the air regularly covered cities in poisonous smog. In a particularly deadly incident in 1952, smog killed roughly 4000 people during the course of one week in London.[9] The toxic nature of using coal for energy restricts its ability to fuel growth directly, and indirectly through high cleanup costs. The more funds spent removing toxic chemicals from coal burning plants, the more expensive the derived energy will become. The higher the cost, the lower the profits incentive and thus, ability to fuel growth. It is also doubtful that carbon dioxide can be cost effectively removed from coal-generated power and safely stored. Even if carbon sequestration is possible, it will be substantially more expensive.

Regardless of how feasible coal is as a future energy source, it will become increasingly costly.

Solar Energy

Currently, solar energy supplies less than one percent of the world's energy. What has kept solar energy at a competitive disadvantage is that it requires a substantial investment in equipment. Furthermore, regions are not equally blessed with a constant reliable delivery of sunlight. On the contrary, most places with a constant supply of sunlight are called deserts, which do not, except for Las Vegas, have a high population. Currently, one kilowatt-hour of solar energy costs about 23 cents, which is approximately 400% more expensive than fossil fuel energy.[10] Even though solar energy is more expensive, it can potentially provide a significant portion of our energy requirements, provided we become more efficient.

Hydroelectric Energy

Hydroelectric power refers to electricity generated by water power. The problem with hydroelectric power is that it alters the flow of rivers and causes a sedimentary build up, which eventually renders dams inoperable while depriving rivers of necessary minerals needed to keep surrounding land fertile. Altering the flow of rivers alters the natural rhythms of the earth's ecosystem; it is not only detrimental to humans but also to many animal, plant and fish species. Without a wondrous technological breakthrough we can expect hydroelectric energy to be a shrinking contributor to world energy requirements.[11]

Biomass Fuels

Biomass fuels, such as biodiesel and bioethenol, have greatly reduced emissions and are a fairly cheap source of energy, provided we are only using organic waste generated as by-products. The problem with biomass fuels begins when we grow agricultural crops explicitly for fuel. It creates a demand for transitioning more of our natural land resources to crop production. This will result in more pesticides being put into the environment, more water being used, and more species of plants and animals losing their natural habitat. In addition to high product cost, there is likely to be a severe environmental backlash. Our biosphere was not designed to be a massive automobile feeding lot.

Nuclear

Any nation that owns a nuclear reactor has the capacity to build a nuclear bomb. The plans to build a nuclear bomb are now sixty years old. The only missing ingredient is the fuel, which a reactor creates as a by-product. When nuclear energy power stations were first built in the 1950's, they were billed as the new 'green' energy source of the future. We have since learned that radioactive 'spent fuels' (created as a byproduct) are not only difficult to store, but are difficult to safely protect from falling into the hands of potentially malicious third parties. The more nuclear reactors we build, the more likely there will be unaccounted for third party nuclear weapons.[12]

Although the world only has approximately eighty years of ready-to-use uranium fuel remaining, there is a potential for more technologically advanced reactors to use recycled fuels and new fuels such as thorium.[13] Nuclear energy could be a virtually limitless energy source.

As oil becomes increasingly scarce there will be an increasing incentive for nations to build nuclear reactors. Hundreds of countries with the potential to make nuclear weapons will create a very confusing and unpredictable future. The bomb that was dropped on Hiroshima was a 16 kt bomb.[14] The current average tactical nuclear bomb is between 200 and 300 kt, which is 5 times more powerful.[15] Experts estimate that roughly 100,000 people died as a result of Hiroshima.

Wind

Energy derived from wind is potentially the most promising of all the new emerging alternative energy sources. Denmark leads the way, deriving 20% of its electrical energy needs from wind. Germany follows, producing 10,000 megawatts of energy per year.

There are several disadvantages of wind generated energy. Potentially most significant is that not all cities are equally blessed in their proximity to a steady supply of wind and the technology does not currently exist to efficiently store wind generated energy. Because of the variability in wind speeds, backup power plants representing up to 100% of the required energy capacity are required in lull times.[16] Requiring a backup energy source in place increases the cost to roughly more than double the cost of coal.

Hydrogen and hydrogen fuel cells

The idea behind the concept is that energy from either coal, nuclear, wind, solar or potentially any other source can be used to manufacture hydrogen. Hydrogen is manufactured by extracting it from water. Hydrogen could then be used in fuel cells to power cars and other machinery. The viability of hydrogen depends on that of the fuel that was used to make it.

Conclusion

It is difficult to make accurate predictions about what the future holds regarding world energy supplies. Predictions vary from complete social collapse to a booming economy based on renewable green technologies. There are many respected experts on both sides of the argument. Any discussion of the costs and side effects of any potential source of energy must also regulate how we use energy.

A 'green' technology may be inexpensive, emit little pollution and have minimal environmental impact, but it may still be used in a destructive manner. For instance, if we use wind power to extend urban sprawl, stealing away wilderness habitats and increasing the need to commute, the net environmental impact may be even worse than using coal.

From a marketing standpoint, labelling an energy source as 'green' is very appealing, but this can be misleading. When society changed from horse-drawn transportation to petroleum burning automobiles in the early 20th century, the transition was advertised as progress to a cleaner, more environmentally friendly future. Technically this was correct. The environment of city streets was sullied by horse manure, urine and the occasional stinky stable, which was somewhat unpleasant and inconvenient. The general public was very eager to buy into the new 'not so stinky' future. The pollution created by horses was of a direct and immediate nature, the long-term, hidden costs were irrelevant.

The use of coal is limited for similar reasons; grey clouds of soot on a sunny day are obvious signs of pollution. If there were no toxins in coal and if the burning of coal did not pump dark clouds into the sky, we would be using it more and releasing more carbon dioxide into the atmosphere. Oil, nuclear power plants and hydroelectric power generators were all, at some point, advertised as new, improved, environmentally friendly technologies. In every case, it was just a matter of time before the hidden costs revealed themselves.

Today, wind and solar energy are being touted as the new 'green' technologies. This may be true in terms of pollution and immediate environmental impact. But how will we use these technologies? The 'greenness' or 'cleanliness' of any technology must factor any and all consequences of its use. The lesson of history is that the cleaner and cheaper an energy source is, the more we are inclined to abuse it and further damage the ecosystem.

Even if we develop a wondrous new energy, completely clean with no ecological consequences, we don't have the social infrastructure to properly manage energy in any form. We cannot continue to use energy to build more super highways, Humvees, yachts, monster homes, computer games and other non-essential items. We cannot keep doing things which grossly alter the landscape, weather patterns, life cycles, ocean currents and send thousands of species of plant and animal to extinction.

Until we evolve socially, a clean unlimited energy source may become an even greater threat.

So what will happen?
As our need for energy increases and we approach peak oil there are two potential scenarios:

1. Energy prices increasing.

2. Energy combined with increased industrial efficiency being able to meet future energy requirements.

Scenario One: Optimism

There is a good probability that energy prices are going to increase.

Imagine a six hundred pound man. He has spent his life consuming indiscriminately and has neglected his precious body. His physical and emotional systems are entirely out of whack; he is diabetic, his joints are strained and weak, hypertension puts him at risk of stroke and he is on the verge of a heart attack due to clogged arteries. One day he finds himself forced by circumstances to go on a diet. This is deeply distressing, but it has its advantages.

As demand for energy increases and oil reserves decline and alternatives remain more expensive, the overall cost of energy is going to increase. The more expensive energy becomes, the more efficient we will become in our use of energy.

Cars

As energy costs skyrocket, it will also become more expensive to mine and manufacture the components used to build cars. High fuel costs will encourage more efficient designs, in particular for smaller cars. The smaller a car and the fewer components used in the manufacturing process the less waste and industrial labour will go into production. Cars will also become comparatively more expensive. The more expensive cars become, the fewer people will choose to own cars, which leads to less industrial waste, less pollution and labour.

Having to drive more efficient smaller cars, cycle or use public transportation is not a catastrophe. In chapter 17 we discuss how better civic design that encourages fewer cars will be an immense improvement to our living standards.

Cars are the single biggest contributor to climate change. Rising energy prices will help encourage a transition to more environmentally friendly modes of transportation. This is a good thing.

Air Transportation

A return transatlantic flight requires an inordinate amount of fuel, producing more pollution than driving one car for a year.[17] The more expensive air travel becomes, the fewer rushed trips people will make. Airlines will be forced to downsize, which will most likely translate to fewer lavish vacation resorts.

Tourism is fast becoming a major environmental threat. Rising energy prices will help not only reduce the pollution emitted by airplanes but also reduce the number of rich westerners looking for vacations in lavish resorts built on previously pristine and healthy ecosystems.

Civic Design

The more expensive it becomes to maintain large streets and urban sprawl; the more inclined society will be to build more affordable energy efficient compact neighbourhoods where people are not committed to long commutes. More efficient public transportation could become an increasingly favoured choice. Basically, the more expensive energy becomes, the less we are going to be employed in energy intensive activities, mimicking the behaviour of our ancestors and other species.

Food

The equivalent of a gallon of gasoline is required to produce a pound of grain-fed beef in the United States.[18] To sustain the yearly beef habit of an average family of four requires the consumption of more than 260 gallons fuel.[19] There is an energy cost associated with growing food for livestock, transporting feed, building and constructing accommodation, processing and freezing meat. This all adds up to a correlation between the cost of oil and the cost of meat. Rising energy prices will encourage diets that are less energy intensive. A diet with more vegetables, grains and beans is the obvious solution. These diets are also less labour intensive. Growing plants to feed people is substantially less labour intensive than growing plants to feed, raise and butcher cattle. About 70% of all crops grown in the U.S. are to feed livestock.[20]

There are 1.28 billion cattle in the world, using up 24% of our planet's landmass. Forests and grasslands are being destroyed at an alarming rate as meat production rises. Animal farming is the most environmentally costly method of food production. It takes about seven kilograms of grains and/or beans to produce one kilogram of beef, and uses almost 100 times the water required for grain and most vegetables.[21]

Our waterways are also at extreme risk. One dairy cow produces as much manure as 16 humans.[22] Multiply that by the 1.28 billion cows on the planet and you have an ecological nightmare. Polluted rivers and lakes are poisoning fish and humans.

Human beings are not genetically designed to eat as much meat as we are. Substantial health advantages are associated with more balanced diets. This topic is further discussed in Chapter 15.

Times are changing and hopefully, we will evolve with them.

Rising energy prices will force us to live a little more in balance with what the biosphere can sustain. It is true that without cheap oil, we can't all drive large cars, eat meat three times a day, live in large mansions and import exotic foods. This however, does not mean that civilization will crumble and we will all starve. It might take a bit of an adjustment, but provided we start working towards increased levels of social efficiency,[23] our standard of living can actually improve. Countries dependent on cheap oil will experience an industrial slow down. Provided the industrial workweek is reduced and work is distributed evenly, high levels of employment can still be maintained.

Worst Case Scenario:

Industry becomes more efficient in its use of energy and more energy sources are discovered....

An August 2005 edition of National Geographic discusses the possibility of renewable energy sustaining the world's future energy needs. Worldwide energy consumption for 2002 was 410 quadrillion Btu and the expected consumption for 2030 is 654 quadrillion Btu,[24] which is a 59% increase. Scientists and governments are hoping to be able to find alternative energy sources to aid in future energy goals. Very few are open to decelerating production of goods. The worst case scenario is that the world gets its energy fix and by 2030 energy consumption increases by 59%. A total of 654 quadrillion Btu is consumed. What could make this substantially worse are technological improvements in the efficiency of industry. If by 2030 the efficiency of industry doubles we will be able to produce double the amount of products with current energy consumption. With a 59% increase in available energy there will be an additional 118 % (59 x 2) increase in the energy value of final product.

It does not matter how clean the energy source is. If anticipated demand is met, we will double the number of cars, roads, factories, airplanes, cities, televisions and frivolous goods. If technology solves our energy problem and the rate of industrial growth continues to rise exponentially we will be able to preserve the status quo. This is the race to the bottom.

This is not a hypothetical example, without an industrial slowdown it is an inevitability.

This equation is formulated in Chapter 11.

Notes

1. Kuntstler, James Howard. *Long Emergency: Surviving the Converging Catastrophes of the Twenty-First Century*. New York: Atlantic Monthly Press, 2005. Page 49.

2. Munasinghe, Mohan. *Energy Policy Analysis and Modeling*. Cambridge: Cambridge University Press, 1993. Page 104–105.

3. The National Academy of Sciences is a non-profit organization started by President Lincoln.

4. Toxicological Effects of Methylmercury. Committee on Toxicological Effects of Methylmercury, Board on Environmental Studies and Toxicology, Commission on Life Sciences 2000, 368 pp.; ISBN 0-309-07140-2; available from National Academy Press.

5. Mercury Study Report presented to Congress. Prepared by the U.S. Environmental Protection Agency. 1997. EPA 452/R-97-0003.

> Because the developing fetus may be the most sensitive to the effects from methylmercury, women of childbearing age are regarded as the population of greatest interest. In this report, an analysis of dietary surveys led the EPA to conclude that between 1 and 3 percent of women of childbearing age (i.e., between the ages of 15 and 44) eat sufficient amounts of fish to be at risk from methylmercury exposure.

6. Health Canada Press Release, *Air pollution kills estimated 5,900 Canadians every year*, April 2005.

7. It is virtually impossible to accurately estimate at what point we will run out of oil and other fossil fuels. There is no consensus

on this point. In addition to oil drilling becoming more efficient, a higher oil price encourages switching to alternative energy sources. One estimate according to Dr. Colin J. Campbell is that we will have reached peak oil by 2010:

Campbell, Colin J. *Forecasting Global Oil Supply 2000-2050*. M King Hubbert Centre For Petroleum Studies, 2003.

8. United States Senate Committee on energy and natural resources. Press Release March 15th.

9. BBC News. "Days of Toxic Darkness." December 5, 2002.

10. Parfit, Micheal. *National Geographic*. "Future Power". August 2005.

11. Suzuki, David. *Good News for a Change*. Greystone Books, 2003. Pages 148–149.

12. Parfit, Micheal. *National Geographic*. "Future Power". August 2005.

13. American Nuclear Society. *Trends in the Nuclear Fuel Cycle*. Organisation for Economic Co-operation and Development. Page 138.

14. 1kt is equivalent to 1 kiloton of TNT.

15. Langford, R. Everett. *Introduction to Weapons of Mass Destruction*. New Jersey: John Wiley and Sons, Inc., 2004. Page 65.

16. Parfit, Micheal. *National Geographic*. "Future Power". August 2005.

17. Mayer Hillman, *Town & Country Planning* magazine, September 1996.

18. Appenzeller, Tim. *National Geographic*. The End Of Cheap Oil. June 2004.

19. Myers, Norman and Jennifer Kent. *The New Consumers: The Influence of Affluence on the Environment*. Washington, DC: Island Press, 2004. Page 48.

20. Rifkin, Jeremy. *Cattle and the Global Environmental Crisis*. Pre-sident, Greenhouse Crisis Foundation, Washington, D.C. Page 1.

21. La Bonde Hanks, Sharon. *Ecology and the Biosphere*. USA: CRC Press LLC, 1996. Page 80.

22. Robbins, John. *Diet for a New America*. Tiburon, CA: H.J. Kramer, 1998. Page 372.

23. The topic of social efficiency versus industrial efficiency is further discussed in Chapter 8.

24. Parfit, Micheal. *National Geographic*. "Future Power." August 2005. Page 19.

25. Appenzeller, Tim. *National Geographic*. The End Of Cheap Oil. June 2004.

CHAPTER 6
OH NO, NOT ANOTHER DOOMSDAY PREDICTION

IN 1914, THE United States Bureau of Mines stated that the U.S. had just under 6 billion barrels in total.[1] They were wrong.

In 1926, the Federal Oil Conservation Board estimated that the U.S supply of oil would last only seven more years.[2] They were wrong.

In 1939, and again in 1951, the Department of the Interior said American oil would last 13 years. They were wrong.[3]

In the 1970s, Dr. Paul Ehrlich, a tenured Stanford biologist, wrote a best selling book 'The Population Bomb' which claimed that by the 1980s, 65 million people in the U.S., plus 4 billion worldwide, would starve to death. He was wrong.[4]

In 1972, the Club of Rome, a respected global think tank, made up of NGO's, scientists and economists, published a book titled *The Limits to Growth* that predicated that the world would run out of oil by 1980.[5] They were wrong.

Between 1995 and the end of 1999 countless experts predicted that the Y2K bug would lead to collapse. They were all wrong.[6]

Even Stanley Jevons, the economist who discovered the Jevons Paradox, predicted that England was running out of coal in 1865.[7]

All these respected academics neglected the amount of available resources and the ingenuity of humanity to find new alternative forms of energy. When Stanley Jevons predicted the end of coal in 1865, he did not anticipate oil, nuclear, wind, solar, hydro and biodiesel energy sources. When Dr. Ehrlich predicted mass starvation he did not anticipate the technology of the 'green revolution' that increased food production by 250%.

Today, as in the 1970s, many respected academics are predicting that rising oil prices will result in the collapse of the economy and civilization. As usual, they are wrong. I am not saying a collapse is impossible; simply that it will likely be a consequence of cheap energy prices and not high energy prices. A rising cost of energy is a good thing.

Although few predictions about economic collapse as a result of high energy costs, have come true, the damage cheap energy has done to the biosphere is difficult to deny. We know that there are less fish in the oceans, storms are becoming more intense, countless species are becoming extinct, and climate change is happening. There is very little speculation required. In addition to scientific research, the effects are easily visible to individuals. To find out about the depletion of fish in the ocean all you need to do is visit a fishing village and ask them why many of their boats no longer go out. To find out about the extinction of species all you need to do is look at the urban sprawl that has replaced their natural habitat. To understand air pollution all you need to do is ask yourself whether you think toxin filled yellow smog clouds above are good for your health. The damage is palpable.

The common doomsday argument presents that without petroleum-derived fertilizers or mechanization we will not be able to meet our current food requirements. There are three aspects this argument ignores:

1) If we start eating healthier, less meat intensive diets we can substantially reduce the amount of resources that go into farming. Growing food to feed to animals and then feeding the animals to people is a waste of oil, water, land and labour.[8]

2) Integrated farming should be part of neighbourhood sustainability. Food should not have to be transported thousands of miles. It is a waste. This topic is further discussed in chapter 15.

3) Human beings have a determination for survival. One of our biggest strengths is the ability to adapt to change. As energy prices rise (hopefully), more people will be involved in agriculture and less people will be involved in the production of wasteful consumer goods.

Sadly the greatest thing that could happen to humanity and the planet is if rising energy prices slow industrialization down to more sustainable levels.

Will this happen?
In the short term energy prices are likely to rise as we adapt to depleting supplies of oil. In the long term we still have a virtually endless supply of nuclear energy and it is just a matter of time before alternative energy sources become more economically viable.

We might very well have unlimited clean energy in the future. This will give us the capacity to completely destroy this planet.

So why is it that we are so dedicated to using energy to fuel continuous growth? It was not always this way and it does not need to be this way. We have the option of slowing down. Before we can do this we will need to understand the role consumerism plays. This chapter examined how we are using energy to fuel continuous growth. The next step is to understand how this growth is dependent on consumerism.

Notes

1 . Gwartney, James D., Richard L. Stroup and Dwight R Lee. *Common Sense Economics: What Everyone Should Know About Wealth and Prosperity*. New York, NY: St. Martin's Press, 2005. Page 43.

2 . Ibid, page 43.

3. Lomborg, Bjorn. *The Economist*. August 2nd 2001. The Truth about the Environment. Page 21. www1.economist.com/opinion/displayStory.cfm?Story_ID=718860

4. Ehrlich, Paul R. *The Population Bomb*. New York, NY: Ballantine Books, 1971. Page xi.

Grewell, J. Bishop, L. L. M. Danly, Clay J. Landry, J Bishop-Grewell and Gregory Conko. *Ecological Agrarian: Agriculture's First Evolution in 10,000 Years*. Purdue University Press, 2003. Page 2.

5. Meadows, Dennis L. et al. *The Limits To Growth*. New York, New York: Universe Books, 1972.

6. Bell, Michael Mayerfeld. *An Invitation to Environmental Sociology*. California: Pine Forge Press, 2004. Page 76.

7. Morris, Julian. *Rethinking Risk and the Precautionary Principle*. Woburn, MA: Butterworth-Heinemann, 2000. Page 16.

Jevons, William Stanley. [1865, 1906] 1965. *The Coal Question*. New York: Augustus M. Kelley.

8. Barkin, David, et al. *Food Crops vs Feed Crops – Global Substitution of Grains in Production*. Boulder, CO: Lynne Rienner Publishers, 1990.

The United States Union of Concerned Scientists has concluded that halving the average household's meat consumption would reduce food-related land use by 30% and water pollution by 24%.

Their website is located at www.ucsusa.org.

PART 3
CONSUMERISM

Why are we building so many malls, cars, trucks, highways, vacation resorts and cameras that can talk in 7 different languages? Is it because it makes us happier? Nope. Owning more stuff does not necessarily increase our subjective well-being.

There has got to be a better explanation.

To understand why we are so bent on our remodelling job of the planet, we must understand the history and purpose of consumerism. What is consumerism? Why have we created it?

CHAPTER 7
THE HISTORY OF CONSUMERISM

THE INDUSTRIAL REVOLUTION, with inventions of steam engines, textile factories, trains and other forms of mechanization, brought about a new phase of exponential growth upon the discovery of the most decisive implementation of the past two centuries: oil.

Oil is millions of years of solar energy neatly stored into an easy-to-transport, relatively stable liquid. Today, virtually everything revolves around oil. Oil is transformed into fertilizer, plastic, pesticide, synthetic rubber, ink and petrol, burned in power plants, automobiles and aircraft. Although plastics only consume about four or five percent of the world's oil production, its affordability is directly linked to the price of oil.[1]

To understand consumerist society, we need to understand its origins and why it was created. Our ambition should be to evolve into a world where the work we do is for our own well-being, in balance with the earth.

Oil is the faith that binds the values of consumerism, and our future is tied to its sustainability. The combustion engine and its most popular application, the car, inspired the restructuring of our cities, casual environmental destruction, and the way we all live. After more than a century of ignorance, it is time to re-evaluate.

The Car – 1888

Although the evolution of the automobile began in the late 16th century, it was not until 1885 that the first successful and practical design made the automobile a consumer viable product. In 1888, the first automobile advertisement was placed by Karl Benz for his three-wheeled combustion engine buggy.[2]

Installment Plans – 1910

By 1910, another brilliantly simple, yet highly significant, social invention made its way into the profit arsenal of banks: the installment plan. Prior to the 1920s, few purchases were made using debt. The high price of cars and the insatiable demand inspired banks and car companies to introduce installment plans. By the mid 1920s, seventy-five percent of all cars were being financed using credit.[3] Debt is a bipartisan commitment. From the perspective of the consumer, debt is a commitment to be able to earn money and thus, a commitment to work. From the perspective of government, debt is a commitment to job creation. This, in part, ties the hands of governments to policies which encourage industrial growth.

The Production Line – 1912

The efficiency of a production line results from specialization. Instead of one or two engineers diligently and painstakingly assembling an entire car, the assembly line sped up the process by having a few easily trained employees specializing in a few tasks they could do efficiently and effectively. By January 1914, brand new Model-T Fords were flying of the line in 93 minutes, ready for a price tags to be slapped onto their bonnets.[4]

The Consumerist Revolution

By 1914, all the cookbook ingredients of the consumer revolution were in place. The general public were in lustful bewilderment of a host of new and exciting 'must haves': cars, silent movies and bubble gum. Best of all, thanks to the generosity of banks and their high interest payment plans, all which separated them from a shiny new automobile, was a commitment that they would be able to work and earn enough money. In essence, consumer debt is a commitment to work.

On a significant side note, France, England and later the United States recognized the dependence of these new products on oil. They began to secure monopoly control of its supply in the Middle East. In 1912, the foreign controlled Turkish Petroleum Company was established in what was to become Iraq.[5]

In 1911, Winston Churchill, in a conversation with Admiral Fletcher, was quoted as saying "This liquid fuel problem has got to be solved and the national, inherent, unavoidable difficulties are

such that they require the drive and enthusiasm of a big man . . . .
You have got to find the oil; to show how it can be stored cheaply;
how it can be purchased regularly and cheaply in peace; and with
absolute certainty in war." [6]

World War I

In 1914, the world was thrown into the most deadly conflict it had
ever seen. Even though wars are socially horrific, they are big work
creation schemes that, in addition to employing people, channel
funding into technological research projects. The governments
of countries involved in World War I funded the development and
application of many new technologies, which would further fuel
a post-war consumer demand for even more wondrous products.
New mechanization skills, radios and passenger-ready airplanes
were all ready to participate in the golden era.

The 1920s: The Infancy of the Consumer Revolution

When there's a will, there's a way and by the twenties there was a
definite will. Will for faster and fancier cars, big screen movies, airplanes that whisk you across the continent and radios announcing
up-to-the-hour headline news with cute cola jingles. The general
populations were not only enthralled by this hypnotic entourage
of products, but were also presented with the means of being able
to afford them, happily trading debt and a corresponding work
commitment. The biggest boom of the 1920s was the automobile
industry. In 1927, 150,000 new cars were sold in the United States.
The automobile industry was the biggest customer of iron mines,
steel mills, plate glass, rubber factories and advertising. As the
automobile industry grew, so did the rest of the economy. [7]

The Great Depression

Even though technology, products and consumers were now ready
for the consumer revolution, capitalism and the free market was
not. The general attitude towards business in the 1920s contended

that government should stay out of the affairs of business. This approach is akin to telling the referee to get lost in a Mike Tyson boxing match. When businesses, customers and workers are left in free competition with each other, they quickly race to the bottom. Businesses can maximize profits by increasing production and reducing costs. The short term result is increased wealth. The long term consequence is that other competing businesses will need to lower operating costs and increase output in order to remain competitive. In the 1920s, thanks to the power of oil and innovation, production was increasing faster than workers' wages. Even though this strategy is applicable for maximizing short term profits and gaining a competitive advantage, it is not sustainable. Workers in factories and fields are also consumers.

One of the few people to truly understand the reasons for the great depression was Henry Ford. In 1933, in a statement before the United States Congress he stated, "We've got to stop the gouging process if we want to see all of the people reasonably prosperous. . . . The factories are not stopped for lack of money but for lack of orders. Money loaned at the top means nothing. Money at the bottom starts everything." [8]

Henry Ford was expressing that due to low wages, relative to output and long working hours, workers were not able to afford all the products they were manufacturing. The less they could afford, the less overall demand, which translated to fewer employees business could afford. Between 1929 and 1933, unemployment in the U.S. soared from 3 percent to 25, while manufacturing output collapsed by one third. New car production dropped by 75% from 1929 to 1932. To make matters worse, many businesses and farmers who had financed the mechanization process over to oil technology, could no longer afford the bank payments. The result was that banks were faced with a rash of foreclosures on farms and business that led to the collapse of the banking system. [9]

Capitalism, version one, failed in 1929 and was never reinstituted. Even though people desired new technological inventions, they quite simply could not afford them.

1933: New and Improved Capitalism

In 1932, Roosevelt was elected president of the United States on a platform promising a balanced budget and a 'New Deal' for the American people. Between 1932 and 1938, Roosevelt instituted a series of reforms which reinstated the role of government in the affairs of business, by protecting workers' rights and financing several large public works programs designed to re-ignite the purchasing power of consumers.[10] One of these reforms was the National Industry Recovery Act (NIRA) of 1933.

The chief architect of NIRA was Senator Robert F. Wagner. In a statement before congress he referred to the wage problem in the following terms: "In my opinion, the depression arose in large part from the failing to coordinate production and consumption. During the years, 1922–1929, corporate earnings rose much faster than wage rates. This led to an over expansion in productive equipment, particularly machinery and plant facilities. The great mass of consumers did not receive enough to take the goods off the market.[11] The National Industrial Recovery Act was based largely on work by two scholars, Professor Rexford G. Tugwell of Columbia University and Harold G. Moulton of the Brookings Institution.

The fundamental principle was that the more inclined the public were to buy goods, the more business could manufacture and in turn, the more employees they could hire. The consumer revolution was made possible by the innovations of the Industrial Revolution, but only became a reality once state policy recognized that growth must be balanced by demand. It would still take many years of gradual fiscal evolution before American and Canadian citizens would be transitioned into ideal buying-frenzied consumers, but this was only the beginning. Roosevelt's 'New Deal', in essence, was recognition that industrial growth has to be fuelled by consumerism; a simple, but very relevant, epiphany that would eventually translate to humanity contemplating its final moments. Consumerism may have been a patchwork solution for our grandparents and parents, but an impending catastrophe for future generations.

1939: The Second World War

In 1929, federal expenditures accounted for only 3 percent of GNP. Between 1933 and 1939, federal expenditure tripled, but it was not until World War II that American and Canadian economies would be catapulted into a boom that would last until the seventies. Between the war years of 1939 and 1944, unemployment fell to less than 2% in both Canada and the United States.[12] The war economy was not run on the basis of free market capitalism, but planned government and business sectionalism. In other words, corporate socialism.[13] The "New Deal" was not enough of a commitment to deficit spending. It took the Second World War to truly inspire governments to bankroll the economy. 240 billion dollars were awarded to business in the form of war time contracts. In addition to inspiring new technological innovations such as plastics, jet airplanes, nuclear reactors and fancier cars, the war also provided a hungry, lusting nation of would-be consumers the means to afford this new world of materialistic wealth.

1944-1970: The Explosion of a Consumerist Culture, Party Time!

From the beginning of the Great Depression to the end of World War II in 1944, the general population had been either unable to afford the big consumer buy-in or was caught up in the national patriotism of supporting the war effort by buying war bonds or serving in the army. By 1944, everything was set to change.

The primary governmental method of keeping the general public committed to their new found patriotic duty of being high-intensity consumers, was by encouraging and financing the biggest work-creating project of the century: mass urban sprawl.

Urban Sprawl

Urban sprawl is not the motive of consumer culture, it is the chains that bind the direction of our labour. The majority of our society can't afford to work less and reduce their environmental footprint, due to mortgages and car installments. They can't live without their cars, because cars are essential to the long distance commutes that give them the ability to earn money to pay their mortgages. They can't afford to read Chomsky, Suzuki or even this book because they simply do not have the energy or sufficient leisure time.

Things are this way because we have designed our cities and the world around us to be as labour intensive as possible. The political and economic objective of the 20th century has been to maximize employment and grow the industrial economy. The lesson learnt from the Great Depression was that industrial efficiency needs to be balanced by consumerism. Consumerism is social inefficiency. It is the inefficiency with which we use goods produced. The most inefficient social invention of the 20th century has been urban sprawl. It has also been the most industrially profitable.

Urban sprawl, the joys of country living in the city [14]

In the early part of the 20th century, escalating rapidly after the Second World War, the governments of Canada and the US have subsidized the construction of roads, sewage drains, power lines, water lines, highways, telephone service, garbage disposal, street cleaning and many other utilities and facilities. Suburbia (in particular, the necessary car support infrastructure) has been the primary employment impetus of the 20th century.[15] Building roads creates jobs for engineers, city bureaucrats and construction workers.

More importantly to the economy than the direct benefits of urban sprawl are the indirect benefits. When people move further out to the suburbs they need to commit more of their labour to being able to afford transportation. The average automobile costs approximately 20% of a person's labour effort. More living space creates a demand for bigger houses, furniture and consumer products to fill these houses with.

The inefficiency that is inherent in our planning and design is deliberate and essential to currently defined social progress. Think about this. Suppose, in 1912, governments decided they would not subsidize the support infrastructure of cars, but instead finance more cost effective electric trolleys, trains and more efficient civic design overall.[16] Combined with more community gardens and agricultural sustainability, what would we gain? We could be living in more efficient cities, requiring less automobile manufacturers, fewer civic engineers designing the infrastructure of suburbia, fewer roads and highways, and smaller armies required to secure oil privilege.

Let me explain this in terms of a personal example. When I gave up my car and started cycling, it also meant that society, as a whole, would not need to manufacture cars for me, civic engineers would not need to build huge roads and, as I no longer had the expense of a car, I was able to reduce my workweek. Consequently, I had more time to relax and prepare meals, which translated to a healthier lifestyle with less doctor visits and reduced medical expenses. Even though I chose an option which greatly improved my life, the choice also reduced the amount of required labour of people employed in ancillary work projects, thus slightly reducing GDP and employment rates. This is what economists have nightmares about.

Notes

1. Stevens, E. S. *Green Plastics: An Introduction to the New Science of Biodegradable Plastics*. New Jersey: Princeton University Press, 2001. Page 15.

2. *Sport Compact Car Magazine*. Honda/Acura Performance Handbook. HPBooks, 1999. Page 36.

3. Alvord, Katie. *Divorce Your Car*. New Society Publishers, 2000. Page 42.

4. Italia, Robert. *Great Auto Makers and Their Cars*. Minneapolis: The Oliver Press, Inc., 1993. Page 36.

5. Ferrier, R.W. *History of the British Petroleum Company*. Cambridge, UK: The Press Syndicate of the University of Cambridge Press, 1994. Page 165–166.

6. Kent, Marian. *Moguls and Mandarins: Oil, Imperialism, and the*

Middle East in British Foreign Policy, 1900–1940. UK: Routledge, 1993. Page 42.

7. Alvord, Katie. *Divorce Your Car*. New Society Publishers, 2000. Page 42.

8. Beaudreau, Bernard C. *Mass Production, The Stock Market Crash, And The Great Depression: The Macroeconomics of Electrification*. iUniverse, 2004. Page 57.

9. Alvord, Katie. *Divorce Your Car*. New Society Publishers, 2000. Page 42.

10. Conrad Black. Franklin Delano Roosevelt. *Public Affairs*, 1 March 2005. Page 285

11. Beaudreau, Bernard C. *Mass Production, The Stock Market Crash, And The Great Depression: The Macroeconomics of Electrification*. iUniverse, 2004. Page 62.

12. Schatz, Thomas. *Boom and Bust: American Cinema in the 1940s*. California: University of California Press, 1999. Page 135–136.

13. The definition of capitalism defines a society where government is separate from business. This description is inaccurate in defining the current interwoven relationship of corporations and governments.

14. Initially suburbia was advertised as the benefits of country living, while being in the city.

15. It is difficult to calculate the exact number of people employed in industries dependent on the automobile, because virtually every industrial sector in the economy is somehow affected. Mining, automobile manufacture, civic engineering, suburban development, and many more sectors are all interconnected. The common link is either entirely or partially the automobile.

The American Automobile Manufacturers Association has the slogan one out of every seven jobs in the USA is automotive-related.

Anderson, Janed. Industry Focus, The Automotive Industry.

16. Design that develops neighbourhood sustainability so that people do not need to travel very far. In other words more small community stores and businesses that are located closer to locations of residence. Three recommendations on this topic are:

Litman, Todd. *Land use impact costs of transportation*. Victoria Transportation Policy Institute, March 18, 2005.

Cairns, S., S. Atkins and P. Goodwin. *Disappearing Trafic, the Story so Far*. Municipal Engineer. March, 2002.

Alvord, Katie. *Divorce Your Car*. LOC: New Society Publishers, 2002. Page 20–21.

CHAPTER 8

WORKING EFFICIENTLY AT BEING INEFFICIENT

SOCIAL EFFICIENCY: *the efficiency with which society uses goods and services produced.*

INDUSTRIAL EFFICIENCY: *the efficiency of industry to produce goods and services.*

Today, more people are working harder, more efficiently and longer hours than ever before. We are task-centric and committed to our role as cogs in the churning machine of industry, always creating more. We are working hard, determined and efficient at being inefficient.

This may sound like a contradiction, yet pause and take a moment to contemplate this statement. It is probably the single most important chord to clarifying the disharmony of our consumerist lifestyle. "We are working efficiently at being inefficient."

Many products are designed to have a short life expectancy. The notion of goods being durable and communal is abhorrent, since this would clearly reduce the overall quantity that can be produced. The quicker a product gets washed away, falls out of the grace of fashion, becomes redundant or reaches its point of planned obsolescence, the faster the market can react to the opportunity. This is a larger issue than corporations maximizing profits.

Suppose businesses suddenly become overwhelmed with sincere concern to preserve the future and, instead of building large inefficient vehicles, started to invest in more environmentally sustainable modes of transport. Are we socially evolved enough to be able to handle such a world?

First, let's analyze exactly what an environmentally sustainable, or close to sustainable car, looks like. As the majority of vehicle pollution is created during manufacture and disposal, an environmentally friendly car would have to be one that lasts a long time.[1] It would also have to be one that uses as little fuel as possible and was as compact as possible.

Evaluating the Consequences:

1. If cars were built to last longer, fewer people would be dedicating their lives to designing, building and catering to the manufacturing process. Fewer would earn a paycheque.

2. If cars are more compact, fewer materials would be required. Fewer mines would be needed to supply ore. Fewer miners would be earning a paycheque. There would be fewer ore smelters, car paint manufacturers, car tire, car battery, and car seat manufacturers. Less oil would be required to make less plastic for smaller cars. There would even be fewer road construction workers.

3. The more fuel-efficient cars are, the less oil they use. The less oil they use, the less people will be employed in building oil tankers and oil pipelines, attempting to clean up oil spills, and drilling offshore wells. We would need less military personnel to acquire and protect oil fields. Hopefully, we may even need less weapons manufacturers.

The net result of a 'green car' is a reduction in overall employment. Suppose, in addition to car manufactures building 'greener' cars, people begin to share. This would cause a further reduction.

The technology to make more efficient and compact cars has existed for decades. The option of being efficient has been present all along. As it reduces gross domestic product and employment, it has not been pursued. Resistance to efficiency does not just exist in the automobile industry, it is ingrained in our culture.

Cars are but one of many examples. Virtually all social aspects of our lives are becoming increasingly inefficient and labour intensive. Even the food we eat is increasingly labour intensive.[2]

What is happening?

Increasing levels of technology combined with decreasing energy costs gives us the ability to produce an increasing amount of goods and services.

This leaves us with two options:

1. We can continue to work as hard. This however means that we have to consume more goods produced.

2. We can reduce the work week. The more efficient production becomes the less we need to work to be able to afford the same living standard.

What is consumerism?

The word consumerism has become a buzz word thrown around in activist circles. It's now time that we give it a clear identity.

Consumerism is the inefficiency with which we use goods and services produced in order to balance production to consumption.

Consumerism is us choosing the first option. Instead of us deciding to spend more time doing the healthy work of community, family, friends, art, music and looking after our own mental and physical health we are doing more the work of growing the industrial economy. We are dedicating more of our labour to work that makes us unhappy and less at work that is good for us. It is not just the planet that is suffering; we are as well, increasing suicide and depression rates are evidence to this.

Why are we doing this?
Things in this world happen for a reason. Rampant consumerism does not improve our standard of living nor is that its purpose. Consumerism is a social invention discovered in the 1930s to boost industrial growth and maintain high levels of employment. The next question becomes why we need continued industrial growth? It is not simply an issue of greed. The best way to answer this question is to look at another social invention from about the same period: the Gross National Product, which is discussed in the next chapter.

Notes

1. The following info is extracted from: *The Environmental Impact of the Car*. Greenpeace International, 1991. ISBN 871532 361

    Manufacturing process involves not just the raw materials such as steel, iron, rubber, plastics and aluminum, but large amounts of substances that deplete the ozone layer, are greenhouse gasses, or use huge quantities of energy.

Iron and steel production requires large amounts of coal and limestone, which are major producers of sulfur dioxide, acids and slag waste. Aluminum Production: involves substantial soil degradation in bauxite mining. Smelters release sulfur dioxide and are substantial energy users. Zinc and lead industries lead to considerable waste problems and a variety of health threats. Copper smelting creates intense sulfur dioxide emissions, while six million tonnes of ore a year have to be refined for catalytic converters in platinum production. Emissions from other pollutants include: sulphuric acid for batteries; heavy metals and VOCs in paints; mercury in circuits; CFCs and other greenhouse gases used in foam seats and body parts and asbestos in brake pads.

Disposal of old cars and car components—tires, batteries and oil further increase the environmental impact of the car.

Cars use 10 percent of OECD plastics production, for a whole range of fittings, from fuel tanks to door handles. Disposal of the large amounts of PVC, polyurethane and high density polythene used in cars is difficult. Over three-quarters of a million tonnes of scrap plastic were produced in 1990 just from cars in Europe. In 1988, 209.5 million car tires, 42.7 million truck tires and 19 million road tires were produced in the USA alone. Over 320 million were sold in Japan, France, West Germany and the UK Of all these tires, only 30 percent are re-treaded, the bulk of the remainder are dumped. Their disposal is very problematic. Heated in the absence of oxygen, tires produce vast quantities of oil, more than a gallon per tire, accompanied by thick black smoke. Dump fires are extremely polluting. Car dumps themselves cause local pollution with high concentrations of lead, cadium and zinc. On average, each dumped vehicle contains six liters of lubricating oils, three liters of fuel, five liters of cooling liquid and three liters of sulphuric acid. 100 million batteries are discarded per year. Their sulphuric acid contents represent a substantial environmental threat. In Western Europe, Japan and the USA nearly 40 million cars are discarded every year.

2. This is further discussed in Chapter 15.

PART 4
COMPETITIVE ADVANTAGE

It's so easy to stand back and observe our consumerist society and think, "Damn, this is stupid, why in heaven's name are we working so hard to destroy the planet and make ourselves miserable at the same time?" It just doesn't make any sense.

The human and environmental advantages of a reduced industrial work week are so logically obvious that this mess seems to be one big accident.

Unfortunately, it is not that simple. Things in this world happen for a reason and often, an evaluation of history and motives is all that is necessary.

Industrial work-oriented consumer-based society is a deliberate and conscious creation with specific anticipated outcomes. Return briefly to the cultural divide in Southern Africa. The whites in Africa, just like their kinsmen who invaded the Americas, believed they were superior. Why? Because they had technology: guns, ships, writing, arithmetic, architecture and countless other sciences. Technological advantage enabled them to conquer First Nations people around the world. The logic, whether unspoken out of politeness or taught in schools was that the Europeans (whites) were superior overall due to technological prowess. The conquered First Nations people, regardless of how advanced their community structures or their level of well-being, were viewed as inferior and uncivilized.

European social and economic ideologies helped create a society with a technological advantage which translated itself into more advanced weapons.

The fourth part of the book will analyze how these competitive advantages are the purpose of continuous growth.

CHAPTER 9
THE DEFINITION OF PROGRESS

The gross domestic product (GDP) represents the value added of all production activities of resident producer units encompassed by the production boundary of the national accounts.[1]

THE FIRST STEP in understanding, why and later how, consumer-based society evolved, is to look at what we are trying to achieve and how we measure our success as a nation. The answer is deceptively easy. All you need to do is listen to our leaders and economists debating success as a measurement of GDP. It is used as a representation of what we are trying to achieve. However, GDP is only an index.

What does GDP really measure?

GDP was first adopted during the Second World War, intended as a measure of industrial strength of a wartime economy. Simon Kuznets, an economist, who originally formulated GDP as a progress indicator, was well aware of its limitations as a standard of living index. In 1934, during a speech to United States Congress, he warned of the limitations to the new system. "The welfare of a nation," the report concluded, "can scarcely be inferred from a measurement of national income as defined above."[2]

What confuses the issue is how politicians, economists and the mainstream media began to represent GDP as a standard of living index. Which, despite being very convenient for politicians, is not the function it was intended for, and is not the function it is currently used for.

There are many obvious and well known reasons why GDP is not designed to measure standard of living. The following is a brief summary of a few of the many prohibitive flaws of inferring the wealth and health of a nation from GDP:

1. It does not value non-financially accountable forms of wealth.
2. It does not distinguish between socially beneficial versus detrimental forms of labour.

Wealth
The Oxford dictionary defines wealth as 'an abundance or profusion of something desirable.'[3]

There are many different forms of wealth. Western culture is in an unending struggle to make enough money to pay bills, or to buy the newest clothes and gadgets. We have come to associate the definition of wealth strictly in terms of money, and in so doing, have discounted other aspects of wealth. Western societies of today maintain a one-dimensional and limited view on wealth. It has not always been so. As a consequence, we have no procedures to account for non-financial forms of wealth: safety, education, community, healthy food and environment, sustainability, art, friendship, and strong family ties. The only progress indicator we have is the GDP. Indigenous tribal populations of South Africa had very little use for money. Community, harmony, music, family, hunting trips and other non-financial measures of well-being were of the utmost importance. As they had no financial transactions, their standard of living index was nonexistent. Post-industrialization, after their land was seized and they were forced into mines, their standard of living (as measured by GDP) rose. Horrible servitude was not a factor. This is not a hypothetical example. The argument the apartheid government used to justify repression of the indigenous black population was that under their rule, the blacks had the highest standard of living in Africa. This argument was indoctrinated into the white population; it was even taught in schools and churches. Technically, they were correct. Today, the same argument is still used as justification for industrialization of low GDP countries. Many multi-national corporations report success from the improved standard of living of its employees who work in sweatshops, such as those in the Maquiladoras region in the Puebla sector of Mexico.

According to the Nike corporation, and the many other hundreds of multinationals with factories stationed in low GDP countries, they are doing the population a huge service by increasing standard of living.[4] The problem is that living standards do not necessarily show improvement, which is a strange contradiction. Generally, labourers in the sweatshops of Mexico were farmers prior to being forced into the harsh conditions of sweatshops. What happened? Mexican farmers were unable to compete with the surplus dumping of American industrialized agricultural produce, which resulted from biased trade agreements.[5] In essence, we are discounting traditional lifestyles values as worthless, because there is no monetary value attached to many valuable transactions.

Not distinguishing between socially beneficial versus detrimental forms of labour

GDP primarily functions as a measure of industrial activity. The harder we labour at financially accountable activities, the more GDP increases, but GDP does not, in itself, evaluate whether the labour being done improves our living standard. To analyze this point, consider a few examples:

Example 1:

A married couple has children and one of the parents decides to stay home to take care of the family.

In this example, the important task of child rearing is being accomplished in the most practical and efficient manner, yet it is not financially accountable, nor reflected in GDP. If however, an expensive divorce transpires resulting in both parents needing to work and pay for childcare, then GDP increases through lawyer and child care fees. Although having time to raise children is better for the mental and physical health of not only the family, but the community as a whole.

Example 2:

Picture a group of delinquent youths from broken homes.

These children are actually heroes of industrial growth; instead of being at home, they are committing crimes that scare citizens into buying expensive alarms, hiring security guards, buying guns, building huge walls to secure their homes and paying taxes to hire legal, police and prison staff. Evaluating wealth in terms of GDP effectively discounts a healthy and strong community in favour of dysfunction.

Example 3:

An overworked society versus a less stressful society.

According to Harvey Brenner, an epidemiologist at Harvard, increasing levels of overwork result in an increase in hospital admission.[6] Gauging our welfare in terms of GDP is not necessarily bad. A society, in which a significant portion of the population is overworked, will spend more money on doctors, hospitals and medicine. The consequence is that we discount a healthy work life balance in favour of increasing the workweek. This aspect of overwork and the 'Lump of Labour Fallacy' is further discussed in Appendix B.

Example 4:

A beautiful, pristine, old growth forest with a rich variety of birds, flora and fauna live and grow harmoniously.

Forests represent a priceless resource in terms of air purification, species diversity, water purification and overall sustainability. In terms of value, as reflected in money and the free market system, it is only worth what an individual or corporation is willing to pay for it. Maximum financial yield is more likely to be achieved by converting the forest into a shopping mall, logging or mining it. The consequence is discounting an almost priceless resource in favour of destabilizing our biosphere. This is why increases in GDP correlate to Earth's decreasing ability to sustain us.

In conclusion, the above examples prove that GDP is not an effective indicator of true wealth or health. Even hurricanes are regarded as good for the economy. On September 9th, 2005, the director of the USA budgetary office, Douglas Holtz Eakin, read the following statement before congress: "Hurricanes Katrina and Rita have temporarily reduced the growth of economic output, but the effects that rebuilding will have on economic activity may more than offset the drag by early next year."[7] As mentioned earlier, even the engineer of this index did not regard it as a welfare index.

If GDP is not a measure of the wealth and health of a nation, then what is it?

Notes

1. Peterson, Janice (EDT) and Margaret (EDT) Lewis. *The Elgar Companion to Feminist Economics*. Cheltenham, UK: Edward Elgar Publishing Ltd.: 2001. Page 411.

2. Hamilton, Clive. *Growth Fetish*. Crows Nest, Australia: Allen & Unwin, 2003. Page 13.

3. Soanes, Catherine, Ed. *Compact Oxford English Dictionary of Current English*. Third Edition, 2003

4. Moore, Michael. Interview with Nike CEO Phil Knight. *The Big One*. BBC, 1997.

5. Amat, Patricia, Mark Fried, Katherine Daniels, Simon Ticehurst, and Katia Maia. *Make Trade Fair in the Americas: Agriculture, Investment and Intellectual Property: Three Reasons to Say No to the FTAA*. Rio de Janiero: Oxfam Briefing Paper 37, February 2003.

6. O'Hara, Bruce. *Working Harder Isn't Working*. LOC: New Star Books, 1994. Page 29.

Harvey Brenner is a Harvard University Researcher who studies the patterns behind the occurrence of disease. In studying hospital records, Brenner has found that the rates of admission mirror changes in unemployment levels. Brenner also found that increasing levels of overwork measurably increased hospital admissions: as much as 20% of all admissions to hospitals can be attributed to unemployment. He estimates that these figures would also be comparable for the effects of overwork. Extract from: Working Harder Isn't Working.

7. Congressional Budget Office U.S. Congress, Douglas Holtz-Eakin (Director). September 9th, 2005.

CHAPTER 10
WHAT THEN IS GDP?

DESPITE THE OBVIOUS flaws of GDP we must truly understand what it represents. For the past 70 years it has been the primary gauge of the success of nations. *It does not determine what we define as successful.*

The problem is not GDP, it is what we define as success.

If GDP is not a measure of the wealth and health of the citizens of a nation, then what is it?

Well, it is exactly what it is supposed to be, a measure of the strength of a war time economy. Gross National Product (GNP), upon which the GDP is based, was developed in the United States during the Second World War. It was developed by Robert Nathan and Simon Kuznets, both employed by the United States War production board. The purpose of GNP was to help estimate how many tanks, planes and guns the United States could produce.[1]

The social scientists who discovered and developed national income accounting during the war were not trying to measure the happiness and social health of citizens. They created an index to measure the industrial competitive advantage nations had over one other.

The underlying principles of GDP remain unchanged.

When George Bush, in his inaugural address to the nation, described the United States as the wealthiest nation in the world, he was not referring to standard of living. Even on strict financial evaluation, the United States (on a per capita basis) does not rank as the wealthiest nation. President Bush was definitely not talking about available leisure time; Americans are some of the most overworked in the world. The average American works eight weeks more a year than the average European.[2] Was President Bush discussing quality of life indicators? Nope, Americans have not only one of the most expensive health care systems in the world,[3] but also one that is not available to all. Americans also have one of the highest crime rates in the world,[4] so he obviously was not referring to a wealth of personal safety. What about education? Nope, five percent of the population is illiterate.[5] George Bush was solely referring to the United States as being the wealthiest nation by referencing the size of the American GDP.

On competitive playing fields of the modern world, nations openly challenge themselves on two levels. The first is on a fiscal level, where countries with the most financial control purchase more resources. The second playing field is traditional military might. Countries with sophisticated weapons and stronger armies have more persuasive power in "encouraging" other nations to adhere to fiscal policy in favour of the interests of corporations. There is a long list of countries which have had the misfortune to discover that fiscal and social policies, which are not in the interest of the United States, attract more than just a verbal bantering: Vietnam, Chile, Grenada, Haiti, Panama, Nicaragua, Egypt and Cuba have all faced brutish music.[6] When a nation spends billions building the world's largest and most powerful army, you can bet your bottom dollar it expects a return on investment, which comes in the form of ensuring policy in favour of American and American-friendly corporations.

A high turnover market, with rapid incentive for innovation leading to mass production, as well as product innovation, is conducive to creating the technological and production framework necessary to build sophisticated weapons. Mass production plus an endless cycle of consumption helps drive technological innovation, whilst benefiting the arms industry.

Although Americans fail dismally when their wealth is evaluated with quality measures, they however remain the most powerful military and industrial nation, without question. They can invade other countries, disregarding pressures from the World Court or other members of the UN Security Council, intimidating and bribing nations into conforming to biased trade agreements, while assassinating and manipulating leaders with little threat of reprisal.[7] In terms of the characteristics deemed most important to controlling interests, the United States is the wealthiest nation in the world with a 2004 GDP of 11,750 billion dollars. This is larger than the combined GDP of all the countries in the European Union.[8]

So what is the problem?

Although the above strategy has been successful in the past, it does not offer long-term stability. The problem of dedicating a nation's labour into driving a consumer-based society, lies in the nature of work itself. If we ignore the important work of family, community and our own health we weaken our society. The United States, a role model for GDP as a measuring stick, has the highest debt[9], one of the highest crime rates [10], the highest incarceration rate[11], the highest per capita medical expenses,[12] and it is also the world's number one contributor to global warming.[13] According to the U.S. Environmental Protection Agency, two thirds of the American population live in areas where toxic chemicals, such as benzene, mercury and formaldehyde, pose an elevated cancer risk.

The world as we know it is changing...

Investing heavily in military prowess to secure oil and other resources is not working as well as it used to. The war in Iraq has cost approximately 200 billion dollars as of June 2005.[14] Despite this investment the United States has not been able to secure enough oil to satisfy its needs. Oil prices have more than doubled since 2001, hitting $65 per barrel in January 2006. Heavy investment in urban sprawl has made the United States highly dependent on natural resources such as oil, water and wood. The prices of virtually all natural resources are increasing. In order to obtain these resources the United States is going to find itself in increasingly tense confrontational situations. The more they go to war for these sub-stances, the more they risk reprisal attacks. War has changed drastically. Technology has left even the strongest Goliath vulnerable to a small country or third party interests. All it takes is one nuclear bomb to severely cripple the largest of economies. Reprisals can come from anywhere: the Middle East, Korea, China, Chile, Cuba, Venezuela, Europe and even Canada. All these countries are going to be increasingly threatened by decreasing oil, water and other essentials. Continuous growth with limited resources means that, at some point in the future, there will be escalating reprisals. With so many enemies and so many vulnerabilities, it is unfortunately only a matter of time.

The United States currently has the largest GDP, but the fastest growing GDP belongs to China. China's economy grew an estimated 9.8% in 2005. Chinese output totalled 15.9 trillion Yuan ($1.9 trillion) in 2004.[15] The industrial economy in China is not the only thing that is growing. China is also potentially becoming the next environmental disaster. Over 300 million Chinese drink unsafe water tainted by chemicals and other contaminants.[16] The Chinese government's policy to reclaim land from lakes between the 1950's and the 1980's has caused lake areas to shrink by 243 million square metres, or one third of original area. Lung, liver and pancreatic cancers are now the main causes of death. About one third of China's territory suffers from acid rain pollution, making it one of the world's top three. As 75 percent of China's energy is produced from coal, which emits about 19 million to 20 million tonnes of carbon dioxide annually and accounts for one-seventh of global emissions, China has become the second biggest producer of carbon dioxide leading to global warming, second only to the U.S.[17]

By 2031, if the economy expands at 8% a year, China's income per person will reach the current US level. Given a roughly equal rate of consumption, the Chinese population would consume the equivalent of two-thirds of the current world's grain harvest and paper consumption would be double the world's current production. Say goodbye to the world's forests.

> If China were to have three cars for every four people, as in the U.S., it would have 1.1 billion automobiles. Currently, there are 800 million cars. To provide roads and parking to accommodate such a vast fleet, China would have to pave an area comparable to the land it now plants in rice, 29 million hectares or 72 million acres. The immense populous would use an estimated 99 million barrels of oil a day; the world currently produces only 84 million and may never produce much more.[18]

In a world of limited resources and fragile ecosystems, nations that work as hard as possible to use as many resources as possible are only gaining a short term advantage. In the long-term there are three major consequences:

1) Irreversibly contaminating natural life support systems.

2) Becoming highly dependent on scarce resources, subject to international competition. Aggressive foreign policies to obtain resources will lead to reprisals, where even the smallest of countries has the potential to cripple the largest economies of the world.

3) A further weakening of community strength. When we neglect our health and that of our communities we foster a weaker society. Real impoverishment is an overworked, tired, and unhealthy population who does not have the personal empowerment necessary to rescue the system.

Notes

1. Perlman, Mark. *The Character of Economic Thought, Economic Characters, and Economic Institutions*. Michigan: Publisher University of Michigan Press, 1996. Page 217.

2. de Graaf, John. *Take Back Your Time: Fighting Overwork and Time Poverty in America*. San Francisco: Berrett-Koehler Publishers, 2003.

3. Organisation for Economic Co-operation and Development: Drug spending in OECD countries up by nearly a third since 1998, according to new OECD data. June 8, 2005. <www.oecd.org/document/25/0,2340,en_2649_201185_34967193_1_1_1_1,00.html>

4. Beirne, Piers. *Criminology*. Colorado: Westview Press, 2000. Page 505.

5. US Department of Education. http://nces.ed.gov/NAAL.

6. Chomsky, Noam. *Deterring Democracy*. Hill and Wang, 1992.

7. Chomsky, Noam. *Rogue States: The Rule of Force in World Affairs*. UK: Pluto Press, 2000. (This entire book deals with this topic.)

8. CIA World Fact Book. www.cia.gov/cia/publications/factbook/geos/us.html.

9. Bureau of Public Debt, United States Department of the Treasury. The debt as of October 4th, 2005 was 7,970,524,003,272.50 dollars.

10. *Seventh United Nations Survey of Crime Trends and Operations of Criminal Justice Systems, covering the period 1998–2000* (United Nations Office on Drugs and Crime, Centre for International Crime Prevention).

11. Schmidt, Steffen W. "American Government And Politics Today", 2005–2006. Thomson Wadsworth. 17 Dec 2004. Page 505.

12. Nielsen-Bohlman, Lynn, Allison Panzer and David Kindig. *Health Literacy*. Washington, DC: National Academies Press, 2004. Page 182.

13. Hanson, Susan and Genevieve Giuliano. *The Geography of Urban Transportation*. New York: The Guilford Press, 2004. Page 283.

14. Academic paper : Bennis, Phyllis, Erik Leaver and the IPS Iraq Task Force. *The Iraq Quagmire: The Mounting Costs of War and the Case for Bringing Home the Troops*. Institute for Policy Studies, 2005.

15. Radio Newzealand. *China growth set to beat forecast*. Posted at 9:32am on 3 Jan 2006.

16. Butler, Tina. *China Faces Water Crisis – 300 Million Drink Unsafe Water*. mongabay.com, December 30, 2005.

17. Hsiu-chuan, Shih. *China's growth harms people and rivers, experts say*. Taipei Times. Dec 22, 2005.

18. Brown, Lester R. "A New World Order". *The Guardian*. Wednesday January 25, 2006.

CHAPTER 11
THE VICIOUS CYCLE

The Efficiency of the Consumerism Equation

EFFICIENT INDUSTRIAL MECHANIZATION, combined with cheap available energy, provides nations with the ability to grow their economies in terms of Gross Domestic Product.

The production of Moai statues on Easter Island helped society develop skills in mathematics, mechanization, writing, trade and much more. The same concept applies today. Production helps societies evolve technologically. In a world of competitive international trade and occasional military conflict, nations with the strongest economies have the advantage.

GDP is often mistaken as an indicator of social well-being. This is incorrect. It is a survival indicator. The inhabitants of Southern Africa probably had a higher standard of living than their European invaders. Well, at least until they were invaded.

The world, regardless of its beauty, is highly competitive. There is an incentive to do as much industrial work as possible, use as much energy and resources and produce as much as possible. For us to understand the requirements of sustainability, we mustn't ignore this.

The Great Depression taught us that production must be balanced with consumption. The more a nation can produce by utilizing energy and mechanization, the more it needs to consume.

Energy used in industrial production
x
Efficiency of industrial production
=
Amount of goods that are produced
=
Amount of goods that must be consumed

Alternatively:

Energy multiplied by the industrial efficiency of production must be balanced with the social inefficiency of using goods.

The more goods and services produced, the more wasteful our society needs to be. In the 1920's, production was able to outstrip supply. The solution that Roosevelt implemented was to encourage and enable society to consume more.

Consumerism is the process where efficient production is balanced with inefficient use of goods.

The Vicious Cycle

One of the consequences of increased industrial production and consumer demand is that it grows the economy. It grows the economy not just in terms of industrial output but also in terms of the technology involved in production. A consumer demanding faster cars and computers drives an industry to develop these technologies. Businesses that utilize the most efficient technologies gain competitive advantages over those that do not.

The consequence of the development of more efficient technology is that it puts us back in the situation where we have a choice.

1. We can reduce the industrial work week, have more leisure time and still produce the same amount of goods.

2. Continue to work as hard and as a result produce more goods that need to be consumed.

This cycle is represented in diagram 1.

Diagram 1

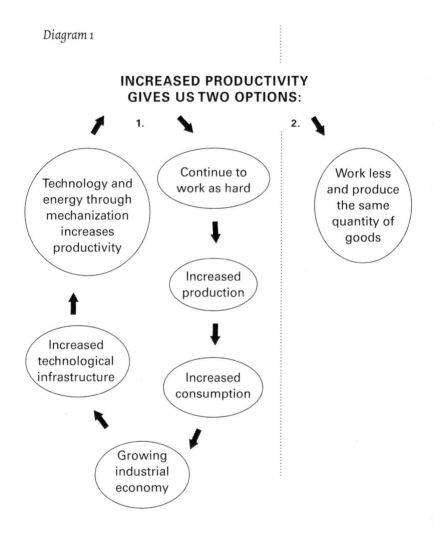

**INCREASED PRODUCTIVITY
GIVES US TWO OPTIONS:**

1.

2.

Technology and energy through mechanization increases productivity

Continue to work as hard

Work less and produce the same quantity of goods

Increased production

Increased technological infrastructure

Increased consumption

Growing industrial economy

Environmental and social collapse

What is the Problem?

The above equation has one very large flaw. It is based on the assumption that nations with stronger and larger economies have competitive advantages.

This is only true up to a certain point.

Endless production is detrimental to the environment, nor is consumption good for society. A point is reached where the harder a nation works, the weaker it will become and the incentive for growing the industrial economy shrinks. The above equation no longer functions and Jevons' paradox, which it represents, no longer holds true in this scenario.

There are four ways an industrial slow down might occur:

1. Energy prices increase faster than technology can increase the efficiency of mechanization.

2. We reduce the workweek. Work less, produce less and consume less.

3. The ecosystems of the earth collapse to the point where the human population decreases faster than industrial efficiency is able to compensate for less people.

4. The scarcity of resources result in increasingly fatal wars.

There is one certainty; there will be an industrial slow down. The only question is how will it occur.

PART 5
AN ENVIRONMENTAL, SOCIAL AND ECONOMIC REVOLUTION

CHAPTER 12
BREAKING THE CYCLE

WE AS NORTH Americans stand at a crossroads. The world around us is changing at a rapid rate. We are able to recognize that the current system of infinitely trying to grow the economy is not only hurting the planet but weakening our society. Despite the clarity and urgency of the situation most of our leaders are afraid that an economic slow down will result in us losing our competitive edge in international trade. The solutions being proposed are all about new 'green' technologies coming to our rescue and allowing us to continue to grow our economies. What we are afraid of is that if we are unable to compete with the rapidly growing economies of China and India we will lose local jobs, resources and influence in foreign affairs. We do not want to become like the many nations that our industrial strength has allowed us to subjugate: Nigeria, Haiti, Iraq, Venezuela, Chile, Nigeria, Angola and countless others.

The problem is that an infinitely growing industrial economy can only be sustained by an infinitely growing planet. The environment has enforced a paradigm shift on us. We are literally poisoning ourselves with billions of tons of pollution and now live on a planet whose biosphere is becoming increasingly hostile to us. We are currently caught up in what economists call a race to the bottom.

We have an option open to us. We need to break the technology industrial growth cycle and choose the option of translating increased technological efficiency into increased leisure time and not increased production.

For many people the thought of a reduced industrial workweek, conjures images of more personal time and relaxation. However, this represents only a very small portion of what a reduced industrial workweek represents. The misconception is that everything besides personal time will remain the same. This is not correct. A reduced industrial workweek will change most civic, economic and social aspects of our communities. Our cities will need to be designed to be more socially efficient. Even the food we eat will become less labour intensive.

A reduced industrial work week is not about working less. It is about working more at building a wiser, healthier and stronger community.

A reduced industrial workweek is an environmental, social, technological and political revolution that will result in greater income equality, more environmentally sound civic design, improvements in democracy and healthier living standards. All these topics are linked.

The first step in this journey is recognizing a reduced industrial work week as a new way of thinking that will change everything.

Diagram 2

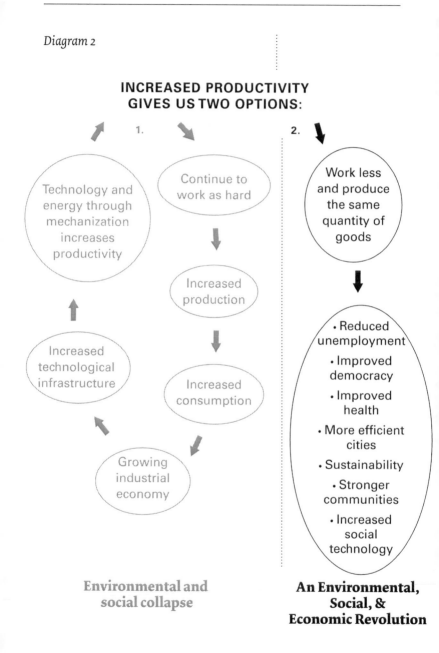

**INCREASED PRODUCTIVITY
GIVES US TWO OPTIONS:**

1.

Technology and energy through mechanization increases productivity

Continue to work as hard

Increased production

Increased technological infrastructure

Increased consumption

Growing industrial economy

Environmental and social collapse

2.

Work less and produce the same quantity of goods

- Reduced unemployment
- Improved democracy
- Improved health
- More efficient cities
- Sustainability
- Stronger communities
- Increased social technology

**An Environmental,
Social, &
Economic Revolution**

CHAPTER 13
MORE TIME TO REDUCE UNEMPLOYMENT

IT IS LUDICROUS that in today's ragged-eared rat race with millions working well beyond any sane number of hours, we also have millions of people in line at soup kitchens, unable to find any value for their labour. Some are working themselves to the bone, while others are struggling to find any worthwhile purpose. Decreasing unemployment has to address both sides of this imbalance.

It seems ironic that working less is a big part of the solution to problems of over and under employment. When I became an advocate of a reduced workweek, I found myself quite regularly accosted in street arguments, lectured by angry left-wing activists accusing me of a bourgeois philosophy, which would only financially benefit the rich and serve to impoverish the poor even more. Provided I was allowed more than two minutes to reply, arguments would clarify themselves. The struggle for a reduced workweek has been central to addressing unemployment in many countries across the world, even in Canada and the United States. It was not long ago that a reduced workweek was the central issue of the labour movement. May Day is testimony and a reminder of the movements' struggle to reduce the workweek. On May 1, 1886, labour unions organized a strike for an eight-hour workday in Chicago. On May 3rd, striking workers met near the Cyrus McCormick reaper plant where Chicago police attacked strikers without warning, killing two, wounding several others and sparking outrage in the city's working community.[1]

Many countries, including our own, have in the past decreased the workweek for the very purpose of combating poverty and increasing employment. In 1933, the United States congress passed the *National Industrial Recovery Act*,[2] which reduced the workday from ten to eight hours. This act was passed to bolster economic recovery following the Great Depression. This reduction was part of a successful series of economic reforms that decreased unemployment, increased minimum wage and improved standard of living. Due to similar initiatives, it was common by 1950 for a single income family to be able to afford a home, education and many other items that we would now regard as impossible with anything less than two incomes.

The reason why a reduction in work hours reduces unemployment is simple. If everyone works less it means there is more work to go around and consequently, unemployment decreases.

There is a relatively fixed useful amount of industrial labour that can be done in an economy: there are only so many pizzas that can be eaten, television sets that can be watched, and books that can be read. I am not saying that it is impossible to increase the amount of labour needed by extending working hours, but that there is a relatively inelastic ceiling on valuable labour.[3] In addition to an inelastic consumer-based ceiling on industrial labour, there is an absolute environmental ceiling. The amount of direct damage caused by industrial labour exceeds the benefits. The solution to decreasing unemployment is not forcing people to work harder, but sharing the workload so that more are employed.

In addition to increasing employment, a reduced workweek also helps increase minimum wage and wages overall. There are two reasons for this. As people in middle to upper income brackets work less, more opportunities to move up the income scale will present themselves. Not only will people have the potential to earn more, less people will compete for minimum wage jobs. This will also help inflate wages. In reality, if we work less, the value of our labour increases along with wage negotiating powers.[4]

Currently, unemployment figures in Canada and the United States are the lowest that they have been in many years. In 2005, unemployment in Canada and the United states was about 6.7% and 6.8%, respectively.[5] With relatively low unemployment rates, it seems questionable that we need strategies for dealing with high unemployment rates. The answer is that they are unlikely to remain low. Due to the dynamic correlation between political, environmental and economic factors, unemployment statistics fluctuate. In the United States, the highest unemployment figures of the 20th century were recorded during the Great Depression of the 1930's and the lowest were recorded in 1953 at 2.9%.[6] As they have fluctuated in the past, they will continue to do so in the future. The fragile nature of our biosphere limits the amount of industrial labour. Commitments to sustainability, such as in the Kyoto Protocol and hard limits set by the environment, will restrict potential growth and, as a result, employment. The last one hundred years of pro-industrial growth strategies are not feasible policies to deal with the environmental crises of the 21st century.

Notes

1. Caragata, Warren. *Alberta Labour: A Heritage Untold*. Toronto, ON: James Lorimer & Company, 1979. Page 10.

2. Raymond L Hogler. *Relations in the United States*. Sage Publications Inc, 15 Dec 2003. Page 126.

3. For a discussion on the Lump of Labour Fallacy please refer to Appendix B.

4. For a discussion on how a reduced work week increases productivity please refer to Appendix C.

5. Statistics Canada, Friday, October 7, 2005 Press Release. U.S. Department of Labor. Bureau of Labor Statistics. December 2nd 2005. www.bls.gov/ces.

6. Galbraith, John Kenneth and Michael Keaney. *Economist With a Public Purpose: Essays in Honour of John Kenneth Galbraith*. New York, NY: Routledge, 2001. Page 194.

CHAPTER 14
MORE TIME FOR DEMOCRACY

THE BASIC PRINCIPLE of democracy denotes that citizens of a nation are invited to participate, not only in the selection process of representatives, but also in defining mandates for each elected official to carry out.

Democracy is not an absolute, it is one of degree, represented by the level of empowerment of the citizenry. Empowerment is about active participation, and lies in the ability of communities to stand up to the challenges of being aware of their interests, and secondly, being able to have their interests represented accurately.

We need to look at democracy as more than an electoral process. Every year, in virtually every state and province the same complaint rings forth, "What's the point in voting? Politicians do not follow through with their promises."

Politicians are able to lie because the general population has very few resources to hold elected officials accountable. Funding a political party or running a candidate in any significant election requires serious financial support. The majority of people don't donate out of charity; they give it because they feel that the candidate or party they are funding best represents their interests. In addition to financial funding, running a successful campaign requires the support of the media. Unfortunately, mainstream media is controlled by a very small number of people with their own agenda.[1] Five companies in Canada control virtually all the media outlets.[2]

What remains?
To run a successful campaign, you need money and media support. You must convince those who have money and control the media that you share similar interests and values to acquire support. Once funding and media support are in place, the next task at hand is to convince the electorate that you represent their values and beliefs. The third stage in a successful campaign is to tell the electorate all the things that they want to hear.

The problem with this conventional election strategy is that you have now made promises to two separate groups.

Which promises do you keep?
If you betray the interests of your backers, you will not only lose future funding, but your face could be prominently displayed on the six o'clock news. Even if the mainstream media can't find a dark secret, which would be strange for a politician, all they need to do is convince the population that you are weak.

How do we change this?
· No corporation or individual should be able to make disproportionately large contributions to political parties or election candidates. If true democracy is to exist, the rich should not have more persuasive capacity than the poor.

· Reduce the workweek.

For citizens to be involved and able to make valuable contributions, they need time. Time to make educated informed decisions, time for access to information and time to become news sources themselves. Time to become aware of the issues and be able to make informed decisions is essential.

A good example of how the media can be used to mislead the population is the war in Iraq. In 2005 the marketing firm Harris Interactive surveyed Americans regarding the war in Iraq. They found that 64 percent of the US population still believed that Saddam Hussein had strong links to Al Qaeda. Furthermore, 36 percent of the population maintained that Iraq did possess weapons of mass destruction.[3] Despite the fact that there has never been any evidence to substantiate any of these allegations, mainstream media was and continues to be successful in creating a false belief of threat.

In countries like France, Germany, Denmark, Holland and Sweden, which already incorporate reduced workweeks, there is a trend for the media to cater to well-informed readers. In nations with longer workweeks, the trend is for information to be presented in the form of catchy headlines and short sound bites. In 2003, when the United States went to war with Iraq, the first nations to openly defy the United States and challenge them on a political front were nations that had a reduced workweek, specifically Germany and France. The five nations with the highest percentage of people working longer than 50 hours a week were all willing to send troops into Iraq. These nations were United States, Japan, UK, Australia and New Zealand.[4] In 2004 the four nations with the longest working hours in the industrialized world were United States, Australia, New Zealand and Japan.[5]

Citizenry of nations, with more time to become informed and absorb information, are less willing to accept unsubstantiated propaganda claims by governments and their media cohorts. When the population is resistant to propaganda, the people who control those media sources will have less sway on the minds of the general population. The less influence the media has, the fewer politicians will be forced to reconcile their promises with those in power of the media and more inclined to fulfill their obligations to the electorate.

Democracy can't function without the population having the time to participate.

Time to become news sources themselves.
In today's rushed existence, where people have less and less opportunity to interact with communities and access different ideas, democracy is becoming more of a cool marketing slogan than an actuality.

When people are at work in offices and factories, there is a strict human resource protocol dictated by the human resource department that restricts polite pleasantry to a number of approved conversation topics and that deliberately exclude topics such as sex, religion and of course, politics. When people are commuting home and to work, they are, more often than not, alone, and the entire outside world is defined by the content of corporate-sanctioned radio stations. Once home, many are dedicated to a rushed list of essential tasks such as cleaning, eating and family commitments. There is no time or freedom to interact and discuss issues that can directly influence us and change our lives.

A good example of people becoming the media is 'Indymedia.'

In 1999, at the time of the Seattle riots in the United States, a group of activists created an internet-based news web service that would challenge business and the corporate funded media dominance paradigm. Indymedia was essentially a website that extended an invitation to the general population to submit news and be the news source themselves. The only editing that was done, was to verify the accuracy of basic facts. What emerged was an international media ring of over two hundred separate Indymedia web communication groups in cities across the world. Today Indymedia has become a daily news source to over a million people. To publish a story on Indymedia, all you need to do is find the time to research your facts, write up your story and push the publish button on their website.[6]

In a healthy community, people are able to share ideas, organize meetings on topics of interest, discuss exciting books with friends, and become news sources. This is the important work of building up a community that is able to challenge unhealthy policy decisions..

Notes

1. Graubard, Stephen R. *In Search of Canada*. New Brunswick, NJ: Transation Publishers, 1989. Page 117–119.

2. This an extract from an article titled "Canada's Media Monopoly", published by *Extra Magazine* in May/June 2002. Author: James Winter:

> "In Canada, five companies, including CanWest, control most media outlets. Bell Canada owns the Globe and Mail plus CTV, the largest private television network; it also controls Sympatico, a Web portal and high-speed Internet link. Montreal-based Quebecor owns the Sun newspaper chain, magazines, cable TV, the Canoe Internet portal, music and video stores and the private TVA network in Quebec. Torstar Corporation, publisher of Harlequin romance novels, also owns the Toronto Star, Canada's largest circulation daily, as well as four other dailies and 69 weeklies.

> Rogers Communications has interests in cable, radio, television, magazines, video stores and wireless telephone."

3. The Harris Poll(R) #14, February 18, 2005.

The Harris Poll is survey conducted by Harris Interactive Inc. Harris Interactive Inc., based in Rochester, New York, is the 13th largest market research firm in the world.

4. Messenger, J.C. *Working time and workers' preferences in industrialized countries: Finding the balance.* International Labour Organisation, 2004. Page 21–24.

5. *OECD Employment Outlook.* ISBN 92-64-10812-2. Published by Organisation for Economic Co-operation and Development, 2004.

The Organisation for Economic Co-operation and Development is a forum where the governments of 30 market democracies work together to address the economic, social and governance challenges of globalisation as well as to exploit its opportunities.

6. The Indymedia website can be visited by going to the following web address: www.indymedia.org.

CHAPTER 15
MORE TIME FOR FOOD

I HAVE EXPLAINED the connection between a reduced work week, democracy and unemployment, but what could possibly be the connection between food security and a reduced work week ? Surely the less we work the less food we have? Not necessarily, factoring climate change and mass deforestation, the reverse is beginning to hold true. The more we work, the less food we have. Food is something that comes from the earth. The more we damage our environment, the less food we will have.

Food security involves three related issues:

1) The food we eat

2) The dependence of agriculture on depleting resources such as oil, water and fertile land

3) Environmental impact
A reduced workweek is fundamental to all three aspects.

Before we address the issue of how we acquire our food, we need to take a step back and ask ourselves, what are we *really* eating?

Food

Many nations, in particular the United States, are facing a particularly vexing crisis. The number one killer in the United States and Canada is not guns, bombs, AIDS or even cars, but cardiovascular disease. The second leading cause of death is cancer. Thirdly, neurological disorders are becoming more prevalent and potentially taking the lead.

The four primary contributing factors to these three leading causes of death are:

1) lifestyle choices, particularly diet and exercise
2) toxins in the environment
3) genetics
4) age

Causes of cancer are primarily toxins in the environment and secondly lifestyle choices and genetics [1] Neurological disorders are particularly interesting because *the primary contributing factor is toxins in the environment.* The maximum role genetics can play in neurological diseases, like Alzheimer's and Parkinson's disease, is estimated to be in between ten and two percent. Bad diet and lack of exercise are not clearly linked to neurological disorders, but toxins in bad diet may be related more strongly than many believe.[2]

We are witnessing an international trend; diseases where pollution is a contributing factor are becoming the leading causes of death. Cancer rates are now almost equivalent to heart disease and, in many places, the prevailing cause of death.[3] According to the U.S. Environmental Protection Agency, two thirds of the American population lives in areas where toxic chemicals, such as benzene, mercury and formaldehyde, pose an elevated cancer risk.[4] According to Dr. Sam Epstein, Professor of Occupational and Environmental Medicine at the School of Public Health, University of Illinois Medical Centre, cancer rates have increased by 44% since 1950. Breast cancer now strikes one in nine women, a dramatic increase from one in twenty measured in 1950. Prostate and kidney cancers are up by 100% since 1950.[5] According to Dr. Chris Shaw from the University of British Columbia, neurological disorders are expected to be the leading cause of death within ten to twenty years.[6]

Bad diet, lack of exercise and the amount of toxins we release into the environment are all linked to our work ethic. The more 'stuff' we make, the more chemicals are released into the environment and the more hazardous waste is left to accumulate in landfills.

In our current world of one dimensional policy thinking, the obvious solution that presents itself would be to simply inform the general population that they should eat healthier and make more balanced lifestyle choices. Unfortunately, this has not worked. Millions and millions of dollars have been spent on consumer education campaigns which have not delivered results. The number of deaths attributable to cardiovascular disease and cancer is still growing.

Education programs are not sufficient in addressing the problem because they focus on the symptoms of the problem and not the cause. Bad diets, high stress and lack of exercise are symptoms of high intensity lifestyles, where people do not have the time to prepare home-cooked meals, spend an hour per day exercising or getting involved in their community. It is impractical to warn people who are enveloped in stress to exercise more and prepare healthy meals on a consistent basis. There is simply not enough time. The problem of cardiovascular, cancer and neurological diseases can't be solved in isolation of our basic lifestyle patterns, no mater how many millions are spent on education campaigns. For us to realistically address the problem we need to make lifestyle changes a realistic option.

In 1929, consumers, with complete faith in the capitalistic free market pricing model of the golden era, were hastily catapulted into the stark reality of the Great Depression and later, into World War II. During the Great Depression and the Second World War, the majority of western civilizations experienced food shortages. Since the production of meat requires a significantly higher investment in labour and other resources, meat in particular, became a luxury good that many could not afford. Most medical experts of the time believed that a diet reducing the intake of meat would surely contribute to a less healthy population and potential outbreaks of disease. Yet, once again, our most trusted experts were wrong. As a matter of fact, the limited studies that are available show the exact opposite. Wartime food shortages forced people to adopt new eating habits. Most people ate less meat, fat, eggs and sugar than they had eaten before. The consequence was a significantly reduced rates of heart disease, cancer, osteoporosis, kidney failure, and kidney stones.

From 1963 to 1965 the International Arteriosclerosis Foundation examined over 20,000 autopsied bodies from different countries. The findings were definitive. Higher consumption of saturated fats and cholesterol relate directly to the rate of heart attacks and strokes from arteriosclerosis deposits. According to a U.S. Surgeon General's report, nearly seventy percent of the 2.1 million deaths in the United States in 1987, were from diseases associated with diet, particularly diets high in saturated fat and cholesterol. This is worth mentioning twice: nearly *seventy percent* of deaths were partially a result of an unhealthy diet.[7]

The financial cost to the Canadian and North American economy is staggering. The Canadian health care system, despite its budget being expanded regularly, is unable to cope with a society in so much need. In 2004, Americans spent 1.6 trillion dollars on health care. Over 320,000 liposuction procedures were performed in 2003. More than 200 billion dollars is spent on prescription drugs each year.[8]

In essence, this boils down to the fact that human beings are omnivores. Despite the meat industry, which includes McDonald's and other meat resellers, spending billions of dollars on elaborate media campaigns showing happy families eating juicy flesh, humans are not genetically engineered to eat meat and other livestock products three times a day. Omnivores are meant to eat mostly vegetables, grains and occasionally, meat. There are many excellent books on proper diet. A simple rule of thumb, that is widely recommended by nutrition specialists, is that meat should only be eaten in moderation and highly processed foods should be avoided. The closer a food is to its natural state, the more likely it is to contain the natural goodness of vitamins, minerals, enzymes, antioxidants, and essential fats. In other words, the more labour intensive a food is to produce, the worse it is for you. Growing grain to feed livestock is several times more labour intensive than eating the initial product. Processing food into strange colourful products, no longer resembling any of their original ingredients, is also substantially more labour intensive than eating the initial food. The more labour intensive a product is, the more expensive it is. The less labour intensive a food is, the cheaper it is. Fortunately for us and the planet, cheaper foods are also healthier and have a reduced environmental footprint.[9]

How do we solve the problem?
First, meat and ancillary industries should take financial responsibility for some of the environmental and social costs that are being inflicted on society and the planet. The environmental ricochets of water pollution, deforestation and climate change are horrific.

There are over 1.28 billion cattle populating the earth, occupying more than 24% of the landmass of the planet.[10] Consumers and taxpayers are footing the bill for these hidden costs. People, who do eat a healthy diet, should not have to bear the financial cost of escalating health care costs and environmental cleanup bills from yet another water supply contamination. It is unfair to burden people with the sins of an industry making a profit at our expense. A tax should be imposed on livestock farming and ancillary meat industries. As the meat industry and most right wing politicians will tell you, the result of such a tax will be that meat products will become more expensive, which is the point; the more meat costs, the more people will switch to the healthier option of a reduced meat diet. Livestock farming in Canada and the United States is a billion dollar industry. Livestock farming is substantially more labour intensive than any other kind of agricultural farming. The less people eat meat, the fewer people will be employed in this very labour intensive industry. A healthier population also means fewer doctors and medical professionals employed. Our unnatural carnivorous diet increases employment in farming and health care. If we start switching to healthier alternatives there will be a reduction in overall employment opportunities. To balance employment, we will need to reduce the workweek and redistribute the workload.

In addition to providing an incentive to maintain a healthier diet, a reduced workweek also helps provide the means. Cooking healthy meals and taking pride in the knowledge of what constitutes a balanced diet is an art in itself. Dedication and commitment to preparing food, and knowledge and caring about food is essential. People have a natural desire to want to be healthy. Our current suicidal eating habits are about as unnatural as our rushed days and endless commitments to producing consumer goods that neither we, nor the planet, really need. Shorter workweeks will not only help people discover what constitutes a healthy diet, it will also give many people an opportunity to garden. Community gardening is a growing practical solution that is finding popular appeal. The social and environmental benefits of community gardens are discussed in the next chapter.

The Environment

The second aspect of food security addresses the feeding capacity of our planet. No link to the environment is more pervasive than our need for food. Each day, as we go to grocery stores, restaurants and take-out eateries, we have the power to influence global patterns of resource use. Think about the sheer tonnage of grain, meat, eggs and other produce that are shipped in large container vessels, hauled across thousands of miles in trucks and packaged in expensive containers. Each step requires energy, labour and infrastructure in addition to the land, energy, fertilizers, water and pesticides needed to grow crops in the first place. Together, these inputs take their toll on the environment through groundwater pollution, oxygen depletion in coastal waters, agricultural runoff, pesticide accumulation, soil nutrient depletion and numerous other problems.

The environmental repercussions from our strange eating habits is an exhaustive topic. There are many esteemed experts in this field, such as Dr. David Suzuki. His book entitled 'Good News for a Change' is an excellent example.[11] For the purpose of this chapter, I will conclude by recounting an experience I had recently with a banana.

Two weeks ago, I found myself in a peculiar grocery store situation. There I was with my most favourite of foods in my hand, a banana. Not just any banana, a well travelled banana that had been shipped virtually halfway across the planet from Jamaica. Even though I had regularly mindlessly purchased thousands of delectable bananas before, what made this occasion more memorable was that the evening before, I had watched a documentary called 'Life and Debt', which highlighted the financial life cycle of Jamaica's number one export, bananas.[12] While holding up my tasty little affordable yellow friend, I had a vision of a poor farmer, picking the banana, it then being loaded into a huge shipping container, loaded onto a huge freighter and shipped thousands of miles to a harbour somewhere in North America, after travelling thousands of miles in a boat. I then imagined the banana that I was holding being unpacked and transferred into a warehouse. Journey incomplete, it was reloaded onto an eighteen-wheel truck and transported several more hundred miles to a large market warehouse. Shortly thereafter, finally being delivered to my favourite corner grocery store, it was moments away from being doused in soy milk and blended with honey into the perfect smoothie. All this for *eighteen cents?*

We have created a very industrial and resource heavy infrastructure to transport food. The further food has to travel, the more directly it correlates to the negative environmental impact it has on the planet. Mining ore to build ships causes pollution, building freighters causes pollution, ships leaking oil into the oceans is polluting, trucks and ships transporting food emit greenhouse gases and other poisonous toxins into the environment, the list of environmental repercussions is endless.

How do we solve this problem? The solution is to start growing and begin eating indigenous foods. Foods that can be grown locally. Once we start eating locally grown food, we reduce the infrastructure needed to transport food. There are many ways that locally grown food produce can be encouraged; however, the result will be a reduction in the overall amount of labour required. When we no longer need as many boats, trucks and long train rides to transport food, we also need less of this support infrastructure that goes into designing, building, maintaining and using all this equipment.

Notes

1. Editors Polyxeni Nicolopoulou-Stamati, Vyvyan C Howard, N Van Larebeke, Luc Hens. *Cancer As an Environmental Disease.* Springer, 2004. Pages 9–17 and 150.

2. Shaw, Dr. C.A. and Dr J.M.B. Wilson. *Analysis of Neorological Disease in Four Dimensions.* Research paper published in Neuroscience and Behavioural Reviews 27 (2003) 493–595, Canada.

3. Polyxeni Nicolopoulou-Stamati, Vyvyan C Howard, N Van Larebeke, Luc Hens. *Cancer As an Environmental Disease.* Springer, 2004. Page 150.

4. US Environmental Protection Agency. Air Toxics Assessment. May 2002.

5. Epstein, Samuel S. Cancer-Gate, Publisher Baywood Publishing Company, Inc (2005) Page 28.

6. Shaw, Dr. C.A. and Dr J.M.B. Wilson. *Analysis of Neorological Disease in Four Dimensions.* Research paper published in Neuroscience and behavioural reviews 27 (2003) 493–595 , Canada.

7. 1987 U.S. Surgeon General report. C.Everett Koop, M.D., Sc.D. Surgeon General U.S. Public Health Service.

8. Press release from the National Centre For Health Statistics in the United States. Thursday, December 2, 2004. Almost Half of Americans Use at Least One Prescription Drug. The National Centre For Health Statistics is a division of the United States Federal government whose principal task is compiling statistical information to guide actions and policies to improve the health of Americans.

9. Kerrie K. Saunders. *The Vegan Diet As Chronic Disease Prevention.* Lantern Books, 1 Nov 2003. Page 49–51

10. Rifkin, Jeremy. *Beyond Beef.* Dutton Book, 1992. Page 1.

11. Suzuki, David and Holly Dressel. *Good News for a Change.* Grey Stone Books, 2003.

12. *Life and Debt.* A Film By Stephanie Black. www.lifeanddebt.org

CHAPTER 16
MORE TIME FOR GARDENING

THE WORLD OF agricultural farming is changing. The rise of the oil economy of the 20th century revolutionized farming and the decline of the oil economy of the 21st century will hopefully, evolve it.

Today, thanks to the power of mechanization and cheap fossil fuels, a mere two percent of the North American population are involved in the production of food.[1] In other words, the labour of one person is able to feed about fifty people. Innovation and cheap oil have made this possible. Machines are involved in every aspect, from seed to harvest. Oil is used to manufacture fertilizer and pesticides. In addition, oil-run machines are used to redirect and transport water large distances.

Pesticide farming has sadly become the norm. The links between pesticide use and illness are staggering. Annually, approximately one billion pounds of pesticides are dispersed worldwide.[2] Organic farming is a necessity.

Between 1950 and 1984, world grain production increased by 250%.[3] This tremendous increase was provided by energy stemming from fossil fuels in the form of fertilizers (natural gas), pesticides (oil), and hydrocarbon fuelled irrigation.

As oil becomes increasingly costly and we begin to switch to more expensive alternatives, the cost to produce and deliver food will increase correspondingly. This, in itself, is not necessarily bad. It will diminish oil-based fertilizer and pesticide use, hopefully replaced with natural alternatives. We will all benefit.

One solution that can help keep the cost of food down is moving some production to the cities.

Growing food is fun

It is strange that this might be a surprise to so many people who spend endless hours trapped inside offices, with no natural light, shuffling paper, but it is true. Preparing soil, selecting seeds and watching them grow into something that tastes better than pesticide-drenched produce is a rewarding experience. Community gardens improve air quality and decrease crime rates, global warming, deforestation and ground-water contamination, while greatly contributing to community spirit.

Community gardens are a wonder cure for a huge range of environmental and social problems. Depending on the location, a well managed 600 square foot plot can yield 540 pounds of produce, which is nearly an extra serving per day for a family of four, for a whole year.[4]

Global warming

Food grown in a community garden does not require any heavy farming equipment, or delivery trucks. If you think that this sounds like a minor saving that won't add up to any substantial benefit, think again. The amount of energy that goes into producing and delivering food to market is staggering. Approximately eight tonnes of carbon dioxide emissions are attributable to producing, processing, packaging and distributing the food consumed by a family of four in a year.[5] The energy yield ratio of the food we eat today is, by any stretch of the imagination, grossly inefficient. A community garden, on the other hand, is a carbon sink that removes CO_2 out of the atmosphere.

Community

One of the most powerful advantages of community gardens is that they bring people together, remind us of our common bonds, and reunite kinships that get lost in work commitments and the concrete isolation of cities large and small. Stronger communities are better equipped to deal with potential problems such as crime and environmental disasters.

Where do we get space for community gardens in a modern day city?
It is easy to find space for community gardens. Most cities have many empty abandoned locations that have been taken over by garbage. We need to recognize the incredible contribution gardens make to our living standards and start active civic projects to reclaim additional space.

The best place to reclaim space would be from locations oc-
cupied by cars. The average large city dedicates around fifteen
to twenty percent of its space catering to the needs of cars. This
is public space that belongs to everyone, yet it is mostly used by
motorists. Even when a car is not on the road, it takes up a very
minimum of one parking stall worth of space. While driving, cars
take up even more space. The solution I am proposing is that every
driver who gives up his or her car, be rewarded with the space
equivalent of two parking stalls that they can transform into a
personal garden. This should be applied so that every household
that does not drive, gets access to approximately two parking stalls
of garden space.

This might sound like a radical plan, but it is not nearly as crazy
as it sounds. In all likelihood, it is not optional. The world is changing and our cities need to become more self-sufficient, no mater
how much we love our little steel extinction vehicles.

This is why the car space reclamation project will work:

- It provides incentives to motorists to use alternative transportation. If we are going to meet our Kyoto goals, we must give incentives to motorists to let go of their cars.

- Reduces the overall cost and demand on road and petroleum
  infrastructure

- Improves the ambience and liveability of the city

- Reduces noise pollution

- Reduces toxic exhaust emissions

- Reduces the amount of petroleum-based products used in
  industrial farming

- Builds community

- Provides healthy food

- Helps residents exercise

- Provides a food source that is independent of rising energy costs

The strongest argument against the above strategy is that cars improve our productivity, but once you factor in the cost of building, running and maintaining single-occupancy vehicles, they actually represent a decrease in overall productivity.

Inner city community gardens are not a new concept. Throughout the last century, times of crisis have reignited the value of community gardens. Liberty Gardens of World War I, the Victory Gardens of World War II, and many gardens which sprang up during the Great Depression helped to physically and mentally sustain our cities.[6]

A good example of how urban agriculture can contribute to national food production is Cuba. In 1989, with the collapse of the Soviet Union, Cuba lost its access to affordable petroleum and petroleum derived products, such as fertilizer and pesticides. Initially, American experts smugly delighted in what appeared to be the imminent demise of their nemesis, but they were wrong. At that time Cuba imported about 30% of its food requirements. With the collapse of its largest trading partner, Cuba no longer had the money to buy either food or the oil needed to sustain its agriculture.[7] Through government initiative, Cubans were able to relearn how to farm organically. In addition to rejuvenating rural farm communities by replacing industrial farming techniques with more communal family orientated approaches, Cuban cities became agriculturally self-sufficient. The transition to organic food sustainability took approximately ten years and was greatly facilitated by a generation of Cubans with farming experience from before the transition to mechanized industrial farming.[8]

If we combine the benefits of a reduced workweek with the benefits of community gardens, we will be able to revitalize cities into fertile thriving centres of art, creativity, beauty and sustainability. The closer food is grown to its location of consumption, the less energy is required to transport it and less labour investment is required in building the infrastructure of transportation. In other words, the fewer trucks, ships, trains and roads need to be built. The closer food is grown, the less damage is done to the biosphere, the less industrial labour needs to be done and the more we can rebuild the strength and beauty of our communities.

Notes

1. US Climate Action Report. Published by the Environmental Protection Agency, May 2002. The United States Environmental Protection Agency is a U.S. Department of State.

2. Pesticide Exposure During Pregnancy: Links to Learning Disabilities, A.D.D. and Behaviour Disorders. www.chem-tox.com/pregnancy/pregpest.htm.

3. Slafer, Gustavo A. *Genetic Improvement of Field Crops*. New York, NY: Marcel Dekker, 1993. Page 3–5.

4. Sommers, L. *The Community Garden Book*. Burlington, Vermont: Gardens For All, Inc., 1984. Page VIII.

5. Building Research Establishment, 1998. Building a sustainable future. General information report 53, energy efficiency best practice programme, Building Research Establishment. Garston, UK.

6. Allen, Patricia. Together at the Table: Sustainability and Sustenance in the American Agrifood System. Penn State Press, 2004. Page 69–70.

7. Peter Schwab. *Cuba*. Palgrave. 15 Dec 1998. Page 79–80.

8. Porter, Philip and Eric S. Sheppard. *A World of Difference: Society, Nature, Development*. New York, NY: Guilford Press, 1998. Pages 201–202.

CHAPTER 17
MORE TIME FOR FEWER CARS

The Justice Minister Visits the Queen, The Netherlands.

CARS ARE THE most ominous inventions of the 20th century. They are probably the single greatest *optional* and *arbitrary* threat to human sustainability.

As with most inventions, a proviso is necessary; the problem of cars is not cars themselves, but rather how we use the technology.

For many today, particularly in Western society, the idea of living without automobiles seems to be a completely outrageous infringement on personal freedom. We have elevated the status of this desire by civically catering to the needs of cars, well above and beyond the needs of society as a whole. Instead of people living close to their location of work, they join daily mass migrations, spending hours commuting from neighbouring suburbs to inner city addresses of employment. Commuters in Toronto and New York spend an average of eighty minutes commuting each day.[1] Consequently, many have become highly dependent on this inefficient, expensive and most importantly, environmentally damaging mode of transportation.

Fortunately, high oil prices are inspiring a growing international awareness that civic engineering should focus on strengthening the independence of neighbourhoods from the demands of having to travel long distances to work. Some cities, like Vancouver and its GVRD (Greater Vancouver Regional District), are recognizing the unsustainable practice of catering to automobiles. Vancouver is the only large city in North America that does not have a highway leading to its downtown core, plus an active city lobbying group that plans on keeping it that way. Unfortunately, building more highways and catering to the needs of cars actually increases commute times and traffic. This phenomenon is known as *induced traffic*. The more highways and roads we build, the more congestion increases. It seems like perverse and reverse logic, but the more freeway feeder connectors a city builds, the more people are willing to move into suburbia and switch to automobile transportation. The majority of studies on this topic conclude that, on average, 90 percent of all new highway capacity added is filled within four years.[2]

When residents make the initial decision to move to the suburbs they normally calculate their commute time without taking into consideration the rapid overcrowding of highways. What was a one hour commute can double within five years. This strange symbiotic relationship has been going on for almost a hundred years. Traffic jams have been the norm for many cities since 1912. As early as 1907 a writer in the *Municipal Journal* and an engineer in the United States, observed that, "though early road widening projects expected to relieve traffic congestion, the result appeared to be the exact opposite." [3]

When a city restricts the access of cars, by not building highways or providing parking, businesses and home residents start moving closer together. Instead of one massive urban business centre, we find many smaller neighbourhoods meeting business needs with reduced commute times and more space for people. A 2002 research paper published in the UK Journal of Civic Engineers reviewed civic planning in 70 cities and concluded that with careful planning, restricting city road traffic did not lead to greater car congestion.[4]

The impact of cars can be summarized under the following headings:

· How cars destroy community
· Why cars are so slow
· High oil prices demand that we rethink urban sprawl
· Cars are bad for our physical health
· The taxpayer burden of cars
· How much space they waste
· Environmental impact

How They Destroy Community

As people move further and further away from small city neighbourhoods into suburban isolation, cities themselves start to lose their vibrancy as a centre of neighbourhood spirit.

The concept of community and neighbourhood spirit can, but often does not, catch on in the suburban landscape of monotonous housing construction. Humans are sociable creatures: valuable and honest interaction with each other is essential to good health and the health of communities. In suburbia, where neighbours only know each other through rare hellos and are isolated by long commutes to and from work, the essential seeds of community are unable to grow. People need time and an environment which fosters interaction and participation. The suburban ritual of work, driving and television is not that place. The spirit of community is priceless and can change everything; once lost, it is difficult to re-ignite.

Cars Are Sooo Slowwww...

I know this is something that is hard for many drivers to believe; I myself only discovered how inefficient cars were once I had given up driving. I stopped driving for environmental reasons. The reason why I never started again was because life is too short to waste behind a steering wheel, slowly going nowhere.

How can this be? How can a technology that is capable of hurtling down a highway at 300 kilometres per hour ever be called slow? Consider the following statistics. The average American will spend 1560 hours working to afford a car. The average Canadian will spend 1552 hours.[5] The time spent earning money to afford to drive, needs to be factored into commute times.

In its yearly "Your Driving Costs" study, the American Automobile Association(AAA) calculates what it costs to own and operate a vehicle for 10,000 miles of annual driving and five years of ownership before trading it in. AAA says motorists pay an average of 68.9 cents per mile, or $6,890 a year, for a 2004 model car in the United States. This figure takes into account gas, oil, maintenance and tires as well as insurance, depreciation, financing charges, licensing, title, taxes, registration and plates.[6]

Example of Monthly Payments:

Your car payments or depreciation	$200
Insurance	$100
Maintenance	$130
Fuel	$120
Monthly distance traveled	1200 km

Monthly take home salary is $2200 for 170 hours of labour.

Total monthly car expense is $550 for 691 km.

Time spent driving per month, including stop and go traffic, is 40 hours. This represents a 25% labour effort to own a car ($2200 / $550) = 42 hours of labour to earn enough money to drive a car each month.

If we add the 42 hours of labour to the time spent driving the car, our total time investment in the car would be 82 hours. Essentially what this means is that we are spending 82 hours to travel 1200 km.

Once labour time is factored into the cost of the car, the car only travels at a speed of 14km per hour. 14 km per hour is slower than what the average cyclist can do and marginally faster than an average jogger.

The above example is a generalization and not specific enough to apply to every commuter, a website that will help individuals calculate how fast his or her car cars travel once labour time is added to commute time can be found at www.worklessparty.org/cartime.

The best way to discuss this inefficiency comes from personal experience. When I stopped driving in 2001, the quality of my life drastically improved. Primarily, because I no longer had the expenses of a car, I was able to switch to a four day workweek. Even on a four day workweek, I still had more disposable income than if I had owned a car. In addition to having more time and money, I was now able to use my commute time more constructively. On days that I took the train to work, I would enjoy a good book. On days that cycled, I got some much needed exercise. By using my time constructively and enjoyably, my commute time was no longer time being wasted.

The Taxpayer Burden of Cars

The automobile industry is the most government subsidized industry in the world. When car owners complain about the dollar or more per litre that they pay at the pump, they are grossly underestimating the extent to which our tax dollars are being used to subsidize the necessary infrastructure required to support our dependence on automobiles. In addition to building roads and subsidizing refinery construction, we must add the hidden costs of air pollution, car accidents, climate change, the military expenditures of securing oil plus countless other hidden costs. Many hidden costs are paid out of tax dollars of people who do not even own a car.

Air Pollution
Air pollution damages the health of millions each year. This

imposes significant economic and social costs. Air pollution is linked to a wide variety of health concerns, including many forms of cancer, asthma, cardiovascular disease, lead and carbon monoxide poisoning, and emphysema. The social impact of air pollution on human health is not limited to medical costs. Medical costs associated with a hospital admission for respiratory disease is, on average, $3000. This figure does not account for the pain and suffering that accompanies such an illness. In a study sponsored by Environment Canada and Health Canada, a mere 10% reduction in air pollution would be of a $4 billion benefit to Canadians.[7]

In addition to air pollution generated directly by cars, air pollution which is created by the manufacturing of cars and refinement of oil should also be added to the cost. Manufacturing involves pollution intensive processes such as metal mining, refining and fabricating, battery manufacture and disposal, painting and a virtually endless list of other environmentally hazardous processes. The actual manufacturing and disposal process of a car will cause more environmental damage and release more pollutants into the environment than the use of one automobile.[8]

Climate Change
Cars, through their production, use and disposal, are the single largest contributor to greenhouse gasses leading to climate change. Every car and light-weight truck emits well over twice its weight in carbon dioxide. A typical passenger car driven 15,000 miles, will emit about 8 tons of carbon dioxide.[9] Carbon dioxide is the primary greenhouse gas responsible for climate change.[10] It is difficult to estimate the exact financial costs of the billions of dollars worth of damage from natural disasters, which are very likely a consequence of changing global weather patterns. Intense heat waves in Europe, Canada and the United States have sparked several devastating forest fires and contributed to crop failures. Floods in Asia, Europe, Canada and the States have caused billions in damage.[11] The three major storms that hit Florida in a 6 week period in 2004, alone caused $20 billion worth of damage. The recent devastation of New Orleans and other Gulf Coast cities by Hurricane Katrina in 2005 was estimated to cost $140 billion.[12]

According to Joseph Canadell, the executive director of the Global Carbon Project, it is impossible to predict all the consequences of climate change, but we do know that because of increasing energy trapped in our biosphere, storms and other natural disasters are likely to be more intense.[13]

Military Expenditure on Securing Oil

Oil is a scarce resource distributed unevenly across the planet. Nations who are able to produce a surplus of oil have a stranglehold on the economies of nations where demand exceeds supply. Oil is a finite resource, thus, nations with a surplus have an incentive to set prices as high as possible, in order to maximize their wealth over the longest possible time frame. In fifty years time these nations will likely have very little oil remaining. The amount of money collected over the next half century is all they will ever reap. Nations with an oil deficit have an incentive to secure oil as cheaply as possible for two reasons. Primarily, it fuels their economies, and secondly, if they did not, oil producing nations would quickly be the richest and potentially the most powerful nations in the world. In order to secure global dominance in world affairs, the United States, Canada and Europe have had a nagging incentive to ensure the obedience of oil producing nations to the fiscal interests of the industrialized world. This is why they have plotted against surplus oil producing nations' abilities to develop nuclear weapons. If they were able to, military intimidation would no longer be sufficient to secure conformity. Even as it is, interferences in the affairs of the Middle East have destabilized the region to the point where the cost of maintaining a military presence is, arguably, exceeding the financial benefits. The cost of the war in Iraq alone, for the United States, has been estimated at $200 billion.[14] This figure does not include the cost of retaliations and increased border security. The World Trade Centre attacks are a casualty of oil dependence. For the purpose of this book, the issue is not a question of wrong or right, it is simply a matter of cost accounting. How do you add the costs of a two hundred billion dollar war, the destruction of the World Trade Centre and the thousands of casualties to the cost of gas at the pump?

The Real Cost of Motor Vehicle Accidents
An Ontario government study estimated that car crashes cost the province $9 billion annually. In 2002, 43,354 people died in car accidents in the United States.[15] Motor vehicle accidents are the leading cause of death of youth in Canada and the United States. Estimates of road fatalities worldwide vary from upwards of 500,000. Each year, 15 million are estimated to be injured.[16]

Environmental Impact of Cars
Automobiles consume over half of the world's oil supply and account for 25% of greenhouse gas emissions.[17] They are also the biggest attributable factor to acid rain, which contributes to widespread deforestation in Europe, the United States and Eastern Canada. Approximately one fifth of coniferous forests in Europe have been destroyed by acid rain.[18] Pollution, directly from cars, and indirectly from their manufacturing processes, contaminates groundwater supplies with mercury, lead and PVC's, plus a virtually endless list of chemicals, the ramifications of which science is still learning. Approximately 29 tons of waste is generated for every ton of car manufactured. Cars are the biggest source of air pollution in the majority of the world's cities. In addition to direct pollution created by the automobile, we also need to take into consideration the environmental damage created by millions of kilometres of roads, which pollute and affect the natural drainage of ecosystems. There are approximately 5.5 million kilometres of surfaced road in the United States.[19]

Time for Solutions

When something is environmentally and socially unsustainable, it means that it will eventually stop or slow down one way or another. If we choose to stay devoted to our love affair with the automobile, then our fate, like another sad Italian opera, will be tied together. If we choose to break this unhealthy relationship and evolve to a healthier world, then we must manage technology in harmony with the environmental prerequisites of a balanced ecosystem.

The first steps to begin the transition are:
· Retracting car subsidization
· Advanced ecological civic planning
· Reduce the workweek and take an active lead in promoting music, art, culture, family, community and sanity

Stop Subsidizing Cars
The labour effort of people who do not drive should not go towards supporting the habits of drivers. Drivers should take sole responsibility for the costs of road building and upkeep, costs of oil wars, increased health care costs, traffic enforcement and global warming research. If the burden of paying for the convenience of driving fell exclusively on those who are responsible, more people would choose cycling, walking or more energy and space efficient forms of public transportation such as busses, electric trolleys and trains.

Build Cities Around People and Not Cars:
This translates to strengthening the public transportation system, while simultaneously building fewer highways and roads. A good example of rethinking civic focus is the Vancouver GVRD plan, which does exactly that. Trains, busses and trolleys are cheaper and more convenient when integrated correctly. Intelligent civic design is nothing new, it is simple common sense that presents many practical answers.

In the 1920s the most popular form of transportation in North America was inter-urban rail and electric trolleys. There were 1,200 separate electric street and inter-urban railways, a thriving and profitable industry with 44,000 miles of track, 300,000 employees and 15 billion passengers annually. Virtually every city and town in America (with more than 2,500 people) had its own electric rail system.[20] Electric street trolleys were cheaper and more convenient than automobiles. Without the direct political and market manipulation by General Motors that changed everything, congested and smog ridden cities, like Los Angeles, would still have a viable inter-urban transportation system.

What the early cities of the United States and current car restricted European cities like Groningen, Karlsruhe and Freiburg

have in common is that they offer a neighbourhood environment of
sustainability. Communities where people can live, work, socialize
and play without having to spend hours commuting in gridlocked
traffic. In Groningen in the Netherlands, 48% of all trips are made
by bicycle. Freiburg, Germany has a vibrant and festive car free city
centre and, in Karlsruhe in Germany, the comfort and affordability
of the electric trolleys are making a comeback.[21] As oil becomes
more expensive, and the social and environmental insanity of car
addiction becomes more apparent, we must evolve to a future that
offers social solutions.

Reduce the Workweek
There are over 600 million motor vehicles registered worldwide.
Automobile manufacture is the single largest manufacturing
activity in the world. It is the single largest consumer of steel, rubber and glass.[22] The automobile is the largest contributor to Gross
Domestic Product. The industry, directly and indirectly through
various ancillary industries, employs more people than any other
sector of the economy. Building roads, highways, arresting drunk
drivers, giving out parking tickets, manufacturing cars, painting
and fixing cars, drilling for oil, cleaning up oil spills, burying car
accident victims, inventing new technologies to make smarter
weapons to ensure our military dominance in acquiring oil, training hospital staff to look after people who have asthma, building
suburbs and second homes; the list is endless. The American Automobile Manufacturers Association has the slogan "What America
drives, drives America." This slogan is quite accurate, considering
that one out of every seven jobs in the United States is automotive-
related.[23]

Directly and indirectly, the automobile industry employs a lot
of people.[24] Even the holiday and vacation industry is dependent
upon people being able to stuff their families into a vehicle and
head to distant locales.

Many of the negative hidden costs associated with the automobile are also key driving factors of the economy. For example, even
though millions of dollars is spent on indirect health care costs as
a result of air pollution, this is money that is being used to hire and

train doctors and nurses as well as commission engineers to build hospitals. Money spent cleaning up oil spills is used to employ people to clean spills, as well as commission research.

The lives of all seven billion people on this planet revolve around Western civilization's consumerist love affair with cars. Change is inevitable.

The advantage of cities designed around alternative modes of transportation is not only good for the social and physical health of its citizenry, but also for the planet. The potential disadvantage is that there will be a substantial reduction in gross domestic product and employment. Bicycles, busses, electric trolleys and trains all require less labour investment and have fewer hidden costs. In conjunction with better civic engineering this change could result in fewer jobs. We can either allow a decline in industry to dictate a reduction in employment, and potentially another depression, or we can choose to allow a reduction in the workweek to evolve our society to a level where more people are employed, but fewer factory and office work is done. If we combine this strategy with a promotion of the good work of living we can greatly improve our standard of living.

Notes

1. US Census Bureau, Summary of State and Local Government Finances by Level of Government: 2000–01.

2. Gordon Price, Councillor, City of Vancouver Director, Trans-Link. "A Local Politician's Guide to Urban Transportation." 2001.

3. Alvord, Katie. *Divorce Your Car*. New Society Publishers, 2000. Page 28–31.

4. Cairns, S., S. Atkins and P. Goodwin. "Disappearing Traffic: The Story So Far." *Proceedings of the Institution of Civil Engineers*. March 2002. Paper 12772.

5. International Metalworkers' Federation. *The Purchasing Power of Working Time 2002: An International Comparison of Average Net Hourly Earnings 2001*. International Metalworkers' Federation, Geneva, 2002. www.imfmetal.org/main/files/PP2004-English.pdf.

6. Jim Mateja, "Cost of owning car rises quickly". *Chicago Tribune*. Apr. 24, 2004.

7. Environment Canada's Website, Human Health Costs: www.ec.gc.ca/cleanair- irpur/Health,_Environment_and_the_Economy/Economic_Issues/Health_Costs-WS085A22B0-1_En.htm

8. Whitelegg, John. *Dirty from Cradle to the Grave*. Umwelt und Prognose-Institut Heidelberg, 1993. World Car Free Network.

McNeill, John Robert. *Something New Under the Sun: An Environmental History of the Twentieth-Century World*. New York: W. W. Norton & Company, 2001. Page 311.

9. Susan Hanson, Genevieve Giuliano. *The Geography of Urban Transportation*. Guilford Press, 2004. Page 283–284.

10. National Research Council. Surface Transportation Environmental Research. National Academies Press, 1 Jan 2002. Page 203.

11. Kunstler, James Howard. *The Long Emergency*. Atlantic Monthly Press, 2004. Pages 147–184.

12.. Holtz-Eaken, Douglas. Statement before US Congress. Macroeconomic and Budgetary effects of Hurricane Katrina and Rita. October 6, 2005. www.cbo.gov/showdoc.cfm?index=6684&sequence=0

13. Global Carbon Project is a shared partnership between the International Geosphere-Biosphere Programme (IGBP), the International Human Dimensions Programme on Global Environmental Change (IHDP), the World Climate Research Programme (WCRP) amd Diversitas.

14. Despeignes, Peronet. "Congress expects $100 billion war request". *USA Today*. 1/3/2005.

15. National Vital Statistics Report, Vol. 50, No. 15, September 16, 2002.

16. Fung, Walter. *Textiles in Automotive Engineering*. CRC Press, 2001. Page 233.

17. McNeill, John Robert. *Something New Under the Sun: An Environmental History of the Twentieth-Century World*. New York: W. W. Norton & Company, 2001. Page 311.

18. Jane Walker. *Vanishing Habitats & Species*. The Creative Company, 2004. Page 10.

19. McNeill, John Robert. *Something New Under the Sun: An Environmental History of the Twentieth-Century*, World. New York: W. W. Norton & Company, 2001. Page 311.

20. Alvord, Katie. *Divorce Your Car*. New Society Publishers, 2000. Page 28–31.

21. *Car Free Times*, Volume 1, Number 2. Crawford Systems, Spring 1997.

22. Graeme P Maxton, John Wormald. *Time for a Model Change*. Cambridge University Press. Nov 2004. Page 3.

23. Holtz, Jane. *Asphalt Nation*. University of California Press, 1998. Page 1.

24. Ibid, page 123.

CHAPTER 18

THE MEANING OF WORK

Your work is your love made visible ... –Khalil Gibran

WORK IS MORE than a nine-to-five mission to afford accommodation and food. Work is what gives us meaning, direction and value in our lives. It is the continuous imprint of our identity onto the landscape of time. The value, significance and reward in our lives are equivalent to the value of that imprint.

Even though depression, happiness and other motives seem to be the driving force behind our labour, they are only the guidance mechanism of matching purpose to action. Cars, extravagant homes, lightning quick computers and money are not goals in themselves. They are only facilitators and, as the world changes, their value in our lives will change. Things of seemingly divine purpose today could be worth less than dust a season later. Today the most important thing might be a shiny new sports car; tomorrow, a sunset with your family, the following day may be the struggle for survival in the aftermath of war. The work we do, in a holistic sense, is that which we accomplish with this life's energy. There is nothing more depressing than to be on the outside looking in on society, where we are no longer needed or wanted. The feeling of being rejected, or of no longer being of any value, is a reflection of emptiness. Isolation, is not just something that happens when there are no other people around, it is something that happens when the value that we have to offer, the value that gives us our individual pride is rejected. Even though, for many of us, our minds have told us that we are islands in pursuit of personal satisfaction, the reality of the interconnected nature of us all is held in our hearts. If he is alone, a king with a thousand palaces is among the poorest of men. True wealth does not stem from material assets; it is value within ourselves and what we have to offer to others. Every other form of wealth is an illusion.

The inspiration to quit my job was a revelation that the work I was doing, between 9am and 5:30pm, Monday to Thursday (I had already changed to a four day work week) was of negative value. Between 1997 and 2004, I was a programmer for Rockwell Software, a large American corporation. Although I enjoyed being a programmer and was earning lots of money, I realized that the software I was writing and which I was, to varying degrees, responsible for was nothing to be proud of. Yes, it was a lot of fun making, but the final product was a computer protocol that controlled production lines in millions of factory plants in the United States and around the world. Factory plants creating products that, after a very short number of years of non-essential service, will lie in landfills. We only have one world and the work we do is our responsibility, for future generations and millions of other species. Even though I was earning a great deal, I wrote software and the software made junk, the junk went to landfills and the landfills polluted the planet. I quit my job.

Today there are millions of people caught in similar situations. They see smog clouds fill the horizon as they stumble to work each morning, and hear news discussing how the planet slowly struggles under consumerist ideology. News of thousands of innocent people dying across the world under a military dogma based upon western ethical structures fills our hearts; we hear news of millions of species of plants and animals on the brink of extinction. People are starting to recognize that our lifestyle choices translate to real environmental consequences.

A real revolution is at hand. Though it has taken many different forms, from anti-war protestors, culture jammers, environmental activists, social justice organizations and independent news groups; all are part of the same struggle. The struggle is one of meaning. We want the work we do, our contribution in this life, to have important and valuable significance. Being mindless office drones, working ridiculous hours that don't fulfill a valuable purpose, is not something money can cure. The news and the decay around us are depressing, while the struggle and determination of people around the world uniting to challenge the system is inspiring. There are more social and environmental activist organizations today than ever before in history.¹ Each day, despite corporate objectives to muffle the news, people across the world are turning to alternative news sources, searching for answers to the role their lives play in the greater scheme of environmental sustainability.

Survival is built into our identity. Without it, we would not have lasted 50,000 years, several ice ages and many periods of global warming. The challenges that we face today are neither insignificant nor unsolvable.

Taking responsibility for your own life

Within each one of us is a world of unanticipated adventure, daring and most important of all, personal growth. A reduced workweek is an opportunity to evolve into a society more capable of thinking for ourselves.

I am often confronted with the criticisms that if we reduce the workweek, people will spend more time watching television. Even though this may be true for some, I suspect that, for the majority, the reverse will hold true. The imaginary escape offered by heroes and villains on television is an escape from boredom and meaninglessness. People with goals, dreams and a real world that embraces them in a true adventure of living, will watch less television. When I reduced my workweek, I had no idea of the incredible whirlwind adventure my life would embark upon. *The possibility of a reduced workweek became a reality* (a reduced workweek was not as far away as it might have seemed), and once I had overcome my personal doubt and resolved that I wanted more out of my life, the transition was incredibly easy. All it took was a ten minute conversation with my boss. The first thing I did was ask him how many people he actually thought did any productive work there on a Monday morning or Friday afternoon. We both agreed that out of 101 employees, only two were potentially productive five full days a week; neither of which was he. He had to dimly confess, that he doubted that the majority actually did any more than three days worth of work. My offer to him was a simple confession, "I don't do anything here really on a Friday. How about me not showing up and you not paying me for Friday?" It was as simple as that. Having one extra day a week changed my life. There are no words really to describe the bliss of having a work life balance that allowed me the time to pursue the rewarding adventure of living life. I got involved in many different community groups, I organized several international protests involving thousands of people and I became a radio host on a small community radio station. I do not own a television and I have no idea what the popular shows are these days.

Governments can facilitate a reduction in the workweek; however, the courage to take that first step can be all yours. For me, all it took was giving up a car. If you look carefully at your life, maybe you too can find a hidden expense not worth the labour investment. Maybe it's a car, a new boat, maybe it's an expensive two week vacation to some emotionally empty holiday resort, a big screen television, a fancy house, eating in restaurants, or maybe it is even all of the above. If there is something in your life that isn't worth the labour you invest in paying for it, consider reducing the time you spend at your current job and use that time to start growing a new more rewarding side of your life.

Changing the role of government

As we switch on our television sets and listen to our corporate-sponsored elected officials dogmatically heralding their successes in office, we find that the most important grading criteria is how their achievements are guided by economic and employment figures. The central issue is unemployment figures, which define the parametres of the slippery rhetoric of politicians, bar crying successes or hiding failures with the aid of clever marketing experts and statisticians.

The fact of the matter is that our society has put its faith in government leaders to guide us. Even with potential cataclysmic climate change, nuclear threat and escalating health care and security costs, the number one grading criteria is sadly consistent.

We need policies focused on reducing the amount of labour required in order to improve social efficiency.[2] Relying upon governments to discover, create, and promote endless industrial work for a growing population is not the answer. Governments of developed nations have proven themselves successful at finding and creating work. Grossly inefficient excess has become the driving impetus of industry, but what they have not been so good at doing is encouraging the important and essential good work of living.

If we define work exclusively in terms of labouring for financial profit, we neglect work that fulfills more meaningful purposes. When we spend time with family, neighbours and friends we build community and social skills, which empowers us with the ability to challenge bureaucratic corruption, to care, to learn and to protect one another. Our mental and physical health is neglected to the point of abuse.

Ironically, many eager governments take credit and pride for proving humanity is capable of remodelling the planet into a wasteland. The role of government in a healthy sustainable future is one that facilitates people having time to do more. Instead of increasing employment through inefficient consumerism, governments should take a proactive approach to becoming socially efficient and minimizing industrial labour.[2]

Work for the sake of it is worthless. Work that reduces our standard of living and degrades the environment is no longer an option. It is time to evolve.' It's time for us to do the good work of music, art, family, culture, community, adventure, learning and enjoying life.

Notes

1. Paul Hawkins, Bioneers conference 2004.

2. I make a distinction between the efficiency of industry and efficiency of how we use goods and services produced. I describe the former as industrial efficiency and the later as social efficiency.

APPENDIX A
CREATING A POLITICAL MOVEMENT FOR SHORTER WORK TIME

IN 2003 A coalition, made up primarily of the United States and the United Kingdom, invaded the Middle Eastern nation of Iraq. The war in Iraq was aided by a well-funded media campaign designed to trumpet the arrival of democracy and vanquish an evil regime. The truth about the war did not, however, escape the attention of millions of protestors across the world.

Many protestors understood that this war, like many before, was driven by the so-called developed world's reliance on oil. Millions of people around the world joined in co-coordinated peace protests. Rightly described as the largest and most organized peace protests in history, the astonishing sight of entire city blocks engulfed by a unified message of peace was witnessed worldwide.

Unfortunately, despite the singing and chanting of war resistors, all of the other cities' blocks were still engulfed by large, gas-guzzling automobiles. People were upset by the war, but very few were willing to look into the mirror and honestly reflect on their role in this war.

Our contemporary consumerist society relies on cheap resources: oil, wood, water, copper, uranium, steel, coal... you name it, we need it and we need it bad. Without cheap oil, we would no longer have 99 cent hamburgers and an endless array of disposable consumer products: from Barbie dolls to nylon stockings, from yachts to planes. The war in Iraq, like many other pursuits in the Third World, was a war for the sole purpose of resource acquisition.

I wondered if there were as many people willing to give up cheap oil as there were to protest the war.

This doubt inspired me, with the encouragement and help of similar thinkers, to form a new political and social platform, one which would examine the purpose of consumerism. We began with a meager budget of fifty dollars, which may garner a small thirty word classified ad in the back of a newspaper. Instead, we formed a political party with an attention grabbing name: The Work Less Party. This decision propelled us to the cover of countless newspapers, plus a multitude of press interviews, generating more publicity than a two hundred thousand dollar budget.

The allure of something humorous attracted the media to us. They were probably expecting a group of fun, lazy clowns who would arrive late for press conferences. Instead we gave them well-researched arguments backed with realistic solutions. In our first election, May 17, 2005, we ran eleven candidates. Nationally and internationally we challenged the fundamental ideas of consumerism.

The charm of The Work Less Party lies in the simplicity of its central idea. Our goal is to identify and clarify the links between environmental and social issues, our current social values, and how they mirror themselves as environmental consequences. We advocate that the solution to our current social and environmental crisis lies in reducing the work week and filling new found extra time with meaningful replacements. It is vital to our survival that people realize what is important in life and substitute replacements, such as family, art, music, community, and health, i.e. work that will add value to their lives. Our proposal: make less STUFF, do more LIVING.

Over the past fifty years, despite a virtual doubling in productive output, the standard of living in North America has barely been able to keep up with inflation.[1]

A reduced workweek is a realistic solution to dealing with unemployment, crime, escalating healthcare costs and most importantly issues around social and environmental sustainability.

I am often asked, "Why create another political party? Surely instead of running in the elections we would be better off if we lobbied other parties to champion a reduced workweek?" Indeed, the cutthroat world of politics has gained itself a reputation of ruthless fighting and purposeful deceit. Why would any honest person willingly want to jump into this cesspool, especially if they had absolutely no chance of winning? The answers lie within the questions themselves. We chose to run in the election because we had no chance of winning, not despite it.

In the 2005 elections in British Columbia, there were three dominant mainstream political parties: the New Democratic Party, the Liberal Party and the Green Party. The NDP positioned itself as a leftist solution. The Liberals had right wing corporate support as their strength. These two political parties represented opposite vantage points of what has become a modern struggle between socialism and capitalism. At the bottom of the dominant triad lies the Green Party. The Greens represented the third component of concern in the electorates mind, the environment. The British Columbia Green Party was one of the most popular in the world and the first in North America.

A neat way to sum up the political juxtaposing of the three main ideologies is to view each as a mirrored concern of the electorate. What did the electorate want?

1) A Strong Economy

2) Solid Social Support

3) A Healthy Environment

The number one agenda item was economic growth. To put it simply, the people of British Columbia wanted more jobs and more money – nothing new here. The playing field was set. All three major parties knew the challenge well; to win seats they had to frame their ideological stance around how their strategies were going to benefit the economy. To win you need votes, to get votes you have to tell the electorate what they want to hear. You have to convince them, one more time, that you are the group that will give it to them. Nothing new here either.

At a debate at the Heritage Hall on May 4, 2005, I remember an audience member asking each of the representatives in attendance: why did they deserve his vote? All three, as usual, swore allegiance to representing the interests of the electorate and fulfilling their obligations of trust once sworn into the legislative assembly. I responded with something different. "The Work Less Party is not here to get your vote, we are here to talk about all the issues that aren't being talked about. We are here to talk about the things that won't get us elected. We are here to talk about continuous industrial and economic growth 'not' being a solution."

We ran, not just to challenge other political parties but to also challenge the electorate. We found that by doing so, we gained the support of not only the people attending all the debates and forums, but also from other party candidates who wanted to talk about more than just financial wealth. Our presence gave them the opportunity to discuss the vagaries of consumerism and the absurdity of continuous industrial growth; two issues that the mainstream electorate were afraid of, but many NDP and Green Party candidates wanted to examine.

So who won? The elections proceeded according to the usual gambit of modern politics; the group that had the simplest message on how they would increase the financial fortunes of the electorate won. However, all three parties had "Economic Growth" as their flagship issue.[2] The Liberals came out on top. As usual they presented the philosophy that capitalism and faith in the free market were the best fuel for economic growth. They promised tax cuts, a reduction in government involvement in our fiscal lives, and freedom of business to pursue growth without unnecessary government restrictions.

The NDP, who came second, built their philosophy upon the economic theory that a healthy economy was dependent on a healthy society to support it. For example, a healthy society needs a strong education system. Industry requires intelligent and trained staff. By funding public education, all British Columbians would have the opportunity to learn essential skills that would make them the productive contributors to a society, which thrives upon smart minds and able hands to support the local economy and compete on the international playing field. Regardless of the truth of this argument, in the minds of the electorate, publicly funded projects have a bad reputation for cost overruns and bureaucratic red tape. What did help the NDP however, was that even though the majority of the electorate was willing to believe in ideology of trickle down economics, there were many that understood, that unless you have a commitment to social issues and workers' rights free reign to business only makes the rich richer. Where does that leave the poor? That's right, poorer. The NDP, thus, had the support of the workers and the trade unions that represented them.

The Green Party found its position quite precarious. How does one advance the economy in an environmentally responsible manner? This issue was and is particularly difficult for them, because they did not have a clear answer. Their publicized position was that a change over to new green technologies would promote the growth of 'green' industries. BC and Canada would become international leaders in this field and more jobs would be created.[2] The problem with this approach was two-fold:

1) The strength of the Green Party lies in that it is a champion for the environment. As such, they should have put the environment first and the economy second[2]. They should not have been debating whether they had the best strategy to advance the economy, but rather should have been championing the environment as the primary factor in long-term economic and social health. Neither the issue of global warming nor it's consequences to British Columbia was raised by the Green Party in the televised debate on May 2005.

2) Many of the candidates and supporters of the Green Party did not believe that we needed more industrial growth.

Here is a quick summary on winning, losing and proudly losing in BC politics.

How do you win?

1) You need lots and lots of money. It is easy to get. All you need to do is make promises to the wealthy. The reliable thing about the wealthy is that they seem to have an infinite appetite for more money; all you need to do is convince them that you can help them.

2) You study the political playing field and find out what are the "important" issues that voters care about.

3) You tell the voters what they want to hear and you convince them that you are the one to give them what they want. Don't

worry if it seems like you have to compromise and leave out issues or gloss over them.

How do we lose the election?

Same as above, except you are just not as good at it as the winners.

How do we lose an election proudly?

Don't try to win at all. Discuss issues you believe in.

Even though the Work Less Party did not win, people were made aware of our message challenging the prevailing theory of dependence on economic growth as the primary solution. We made front-page news in many local newspapers – *The Westender*, the Metro and Surrey Now. *The Vancouver Sun* described us as a new and improved Green Party; the *Georgia Straight* endorsed one of our candidates as the most qualified to win the West Vancouver riding. BC Business magazine did a 3000-word story debating our reduced workweek platform. In a very short space of time and thanks to a substantial amount of support from overworked television, newspaper and radio reporters, the Work Less Party became a household name in British Columbia.[3]

Every state and province, in both Canada and the United States, should have fringe politics, existing solely to challenge the electorate and mainstream polities to think about more than just winning votes and making empty promises. These parties can be effective because they have nothing to loose.

Notes

1. Statistics Canada, January 2005 report, Are good jobs disappearing in Canada?.

Centre on Budget and Policy Priorities, Federal Minimum Wage Remains Unchanged for Eighth Straight Year, Falls to 56-Year Low Relative to the Average Wage By Jared Bernstein and Isaac Shapiro

2. The Vancouver public library keeps an archive of past Green Party, NDP and Liberal promotional pamphlets. Samples of which can be viewed by visiting www.worklessparty.org/book

3. To view this archive of newspaper and television footage, please visit www.worklessparty.org.

Statistics Canada, 'Are good jobs disappearing in Canada?', 1981 to 2004.

APPENDIX B
DEBUNKING THE LUMP OF LABOUR FALLACY

A COMMON ARGUMENT opposing the benefits of a reduced work-week is the lump of labour fallacy, which asserts there is not a fixed amount of labour and as such, it is not possible to reduce unemployment by decreasing the workweek. This theory was named in 1891 by economist, D.F. Schloss.[1]

I am not contending this fallacy. It is possible to increase the overall amount of industrial labour required in a society by increasing the workweek. The problem, however, is with the types of labour encouraged and how they are accounted for. Instead of investigating this problem from a supply perspective, approach it from a demand perspective. In other words, what types of industry does an overworked labour force create? An overworked society:

- has less time for cooking, which creates employment opportunities for restaurants and pre-prepared meals

- employment opportunities for daycare and babysitters abound with parents unable to meet the full demands of parenthood

- has less free time and fewer vacation days and are thus more inclined to want their "leisure" time to be as luxurious and entertaining as possible, creating hospitality and tourism opportunities

- is full of stress and, as a consequence, has higher health care costs. This creates employment opportunities for doctors, hospitals and pharmacists

- has minimal time for community and family. This may result in higher crime rates and juvenile delinquency. Thus, employment opportunities for police and law enforcement officials are born.

The demands of an overworked society are concentrated upon unnecessary industries. Even though it is possible to increase the overall quantity of industrial labour required in a society, there is a more rigid ceiling on the quantity of useful labour.

The lump of labour fallacy also has a major limitation in its application. It uses the concept of work to largely refer to industrial and financially accountable labour. In Chapter 2 we explained that work is something that is always being done, regardless of whether it generates income or not.

Although having an overworked population may result in more people being employed in restaurants and in daycares, it does not necessarily mean that more work is being done.

Example 1
If I look after my own children, the very important work of childcare is being done even though it is not financially accounted for. If however I am overworked and spend money on daycare, a financially measurable transaction is occurring. In both cases the same amount of work is being done. The difference is that in the latter case we have the illusion that the economy is growing because more money is changing hands. In truth, all that has happened is the financially priceless (in more ways than one) work of parenting being swapped with financially measurable work of daycare.

Having an overworked labour force reduces the time people have for looking after their own personal needs and thus, creates an industry to serve this purpose. As these industries are financially measurable it creates the illusion of growth. In comparison, the work of living is not financially accounted for.

Notes

1. Walker, Tom. "The 'Lump-Of Labour' case against work sharing". Routledge Press. 2000. Page 7

For more information on the arguments against the 'lump of labour fallacy', I recommend reading some of the papers written by Tom Walker. I have put downloadable copies of his papers on the following website. www.WorkersOfTheWorldRelax.org/book/tom.

The above discussion on the lump of labour fallacy is by no means complete. A substantial amount of research still needs to be done on this topic.

APPENDIX C
INCREASES IN PRODUCTIVITY

THERE HAVE BEEN a number of studies, dating back to 1893, which have shown that a reduction in the number of daily work hours increases per hour productivity rate.[1]

In 1926, when Henry Ford adopted the forty hour workweek, production costs decreased and overall output increased. The 1997 reduction of the workweek in France resulted in an increase in productivity, as well as a decrease in unemployment. According to France's national planning agency, work-time reduction helped bring unemployment down from 12.5% in 1997 to an eighteen-year low of 8.6% in 2001.[2]

France's workweek reduction was financed by an increase in worker productivity, combined with an increase in the number of people employed. The more people that are actively contributing to the economy, the less the financial tax burden on those who are working.[3]

If wages are a function of output, then increasing per hour productivity will result in an increase in wages. However, for a reduced workweek to be an effective solution to reducing our environmental footprint, there needs to be a reduction in overall goods produced and, as such, the hours worked have to be reduced to beyond the point where a decrease in output is no longer offset by gains in per hour productivity and increases in employment. In other words, for there to be a reduction in output, the cost of hiring, training and managing employees needs to exceed the benefit of increased productivity and increased employment.

As the value of money is determined by the number of goods and services it can buy, a reduction in output will result in a decrease in purchasing power. Attempting to pay people the same amount of money for reduced output will only result in inflation.

Provided we have a reduction in output, the personal financial consequence of a reduction of the workweek will result in an increase in wages, but a net reduction in take home pay. Despite the fact that it would be a popular promotional campaign to promise a reduced workweek without a reduction in pay, it would not be possible if there is a reduction in output. If our goal is to reduce our environmental footprint there must be a net decrease in industrial output.

Notes

1. Sidney J. Chapman's 1909 address on the "Hours of Labour" was considered the "classical statement of the theory of 'hours' in a free market", (J.R. Hicks, Theory of Wages, 1932).

2. Anders, Hayden. "Europe's Work-Time Alternatives". Published in the *Take Back Your Time Handbook*. USA: Berrett-Koehler, September 2001.

3. Anders, Hayden. *Sharing the Work, Sparing the Planet*. Sydney: Pluto Press,1999. Page 136–137.

APPENDIX D
THE ROSETO EFFECT

STEWART WOLF, MD, began studying the tiny town of Roseto, Pennsylvania, in the 1950's because its residents were so healthy. He wondered why they hardly ever had heart attacks and lived so much longer than people in neighbouring towns. At first, he suspected diet. But no, the Rosetans ate a lot of pasta and fat. In fact, they were so poor they used lard instead of olive oil. They didn't really exercise more than their neighbours either.

In time, Wolf came to a surprising conclusion. Rosetans regularly lived into their 80's because these poor immigrants, all from the same village in Italy, truly practiced community. They shared what they had, helped each other and frowned on conspicuous consumption – what they referred to as "putting on the dog." Their close-knit families and friendships literally kept them healthy.

This finding, that strong human bonds are perhaps the leading predictor of good health, is now known as "the Roseto Effect" in public health circles.

But, sadly, the Roseto story has an unhappy ending. In the 1950s, Wolf began to worry that the next generation of Rosetans was adopting a keep-up-with-the-Joneses philosophy of neighbouring communities. When he studied Roseto a generation later, the old intimate community had vanished, and so had its health advantage. These days, Rosetans don't live any longer than anyone else.[1]

Notes

1. The above is an extraction from "Life Balance: Achievement Overload" written by John de Graaf.

John de Graaf is the national coordinator for Take Back Your Time (www.timeday.org), an organization working to increase awareness of time poverty and overwork in America, and coauthor of Affluenza: The All-Consuming Epidemic (Berrett-Koehler Publishers, 2005).